THEMATIC UNIT
Wolves

By Linda J. Larsen
Illustrated by Agi Palinay
Cover Art by Kathy Bruce

Bleicher

Teacher Created Materials, Inc.
P.O. Box 1214
Huntington Beach, CA 92647

©*1994 Teacher Created Materials, Inc.*
Made in U.S.A.
ISBN 1-55734-583-X

Table of Contents

Introduction

Wolves contains a captivating whole language, thematic unit about wolves. Its 80 reproducible pages are filled with a wide variety of lesson ideas designed for use with intermediate and junior high school students. At its core are three high-quality literature selections, *Julie of the Wolves, The Call of the Wild*, and *Kävik the Wolf Dog*. These are high-interest adventure stories that transport students to Alaska and the Arctic.

There are activities included for each literature selection which set the stage for reading, encourage enjoyment of the book, and extend the concepts learned. The theme is connected to the curriculum with activities in language arts (including writing), science, math, social studies, art, and life skills. Many of these activities encourage cooperative learning. The unit management tools include suggestions for a research center and bulletin boards. These provide students with the opportunity to synthesize their knowledge and create products that can be shared with others.

This thematic unit includes:

❏ **literature selections** – summaries of three books with related lessons and repro – ducible pages that cross the curriculum

❏ **planning guides** – suggestions for sequencing lessons and activities throughout the unit

❏ **writing ideas** – writing activities across the curriculum, including making books

❏ **curriculum connections** – in language arts, science, math, social studies, art, and life skills

❏ **group projects** – to encourage cooperative learning

❏ **culminating activities** – which require students to synthesize their learning and create products that can be shared with others

❏ **a bibliography** – suggested additional fiction and nonfiction books, videos, computer programs, and teacher resources

---

To keep this valuable resource intact so that it can be used year after year you may wish to punch holes in the pages and store them in a three – ring binder.

Introduction *(cont.)*

Why Whole Language?

A whole language approach involves children in using all modes of communication: reading, writing, listening, observing, illustrating, experiencing, and doing. Communication skills are interconnected and integrated into lessons that emphasize the whole of language rather than isolating its parts. The lessons revolve around selected literature. Reading is not taught as a separate subject from writing and spelling, for example. A child reads, writes, speaks, listens, and thinks in response to a literature experience introduced by the teacher. In this way, language skills grow naturally, stimulated by involvement and interest in the topic at hand.

Why Thematic Planning?

One very useful tool for implementing an integrated whole language program is thematic planning. By choosing a theme with correlative literature selections for a unit of study, a teacher can plan activities throughout the day that lead to a cohesive, in-depth study of the topic. Students will be practicing and applying their skills in meaningful contexts. Consequently, they will tend to learn and retain more. Both teachers and students will be freed from a day that is broken into unrelated segments of isolated drill and practice.

Why Cooperative Learning?

Besides academic skills and content, students need to learn social skills. No longer can this area of development be taken for granted. Students must learn to work cooperatively in groups in order to function well in modern society. Group activities should be a regular part of school life and teachers should consciously include social objectives as well as academic objectives in their planning. The teacher should clarify and monitor the qualities of good group interaction, just as he/she would clarify and monitor the academic goals of the project.

Why Big Books?

An excellent cooperative, whole language activity is the production of Big Books. Groups of students or the whole class, can apply their language skills, content knowledge, and creativity to produce a Big Book that can become a part of the classroom library to be read and reread. These books make excellent culminating projects for sharing beyond the classroom with parents, librarians, and others. Big Books can be produced in many ways, and this thematic unit book includes directions for several methods you may choose.

Julie of the Wolves

by Jean Craighead George

Summary

A thirteen-year-old Eskimo girl, Miyax, runs away from home. She is heading for San Francisco, where her pen-pal, Amy, lives. But Miyax becomes lost in the Alaskan wilderness. She does not have a compass, so she does not know which direction she is traveling. Without food she will die. However, she is slowly accepted by a pack of wolves. With their help, Miyax struggles to survive each day. This book tells a wonderful story about traditional Eskimo life, courage, and a respect for animals.

The outline shown below is a suggested plan for using the various activities that are presented in this unit. You should adapt these ideas to fit your own classroom situation.

Sample Plan

Lesson 1

- Introduce Alaska (page 6,#3) and the Eskimo way of life (pages 13-15).
- Present background information about wolves (pages 47-49).
- Choose one or more of the Setting the Stage activities (pages 6-7).
- Introduce the vocabulary list for pages 5-25 (page 9).
- Choose a vocabulary activity (page 42).

Lesson 2

- Read pages 5-25 in *Julie of the Wolves*. Begin a class diary (page 7).
- Choose one or more of the Enjoying the Book activities (page 7).
- Write a "found" poem using this part of the story (page 39).
- Introduce the vocabulary list for pages 25-49 (page 9).
- Choose a vocabulary activity (page 42).

Lesson 3

- Read pages 25-49.
- Add new information to the class diary (page 7,#1).
- Continue working on Enjoying the Book activities (page 7).

- Introduce the vocabulary list for pages 49-70 (page 9).
- Choose a vocabulary activity (page 42).

Lesson 4

- Read pages 49-70.
- Add new information to the class diary (page 7,#1).
- Discuss Part I (page 10).
- Convert to metric measurements (page 59).
- Introduce the vocabulary list for pages 75-88 (page 9).
- Choose a vocabulary activity (page 42).

Lesson 5

- Read pages 75-88.
- Add new information to the class diary (page 7,#1).
- Focus on language arts skills (page 11).
- Continue working on Enjoying the Book activities (page 7).
- Learn about habitats (pages 68-69).
- Introduce the vocabulary list for pages 88-104 (page 9).
- Choose a vocabulary activity (page 42).

Sample Plan *(cont.)*

Lesson 6

- Read pages 88-104.
- Add new information to class diary (page 7,#1).
- Discuss Part II (page 10).
- Diagram the life cycle of a wolf (page 50).
- Introduce the vocabulary list for pages 109-129 (page 9).
- Choose a vocabulary activity (page 42).

Lesson 7

- Read pages 109-129.
- Add new information to the class diary (page 7,#1).
- Retell the story of "The Boy Who Cried Wolf" (page 41).
- Introduce the vocabulary list for pages 129-147 (page 9).
- Choose a vocabulary activity (page 42).

Lesson 8

- Read pages 129-147.
- Add new information to the class diary (page 7,#1).

- Write a letter about wildlife conservation (pages 45-46).
- Complete Enjoying the Book activities (page 7).
- Introduce the vocabulary list for pages 147-170 (page 9).
- Choose a vocabulary activity (page 42).

Lesson 9

- Read pages 147-170 to finish the book.
- Complete the class diary (page 7,#1).
- Discuss Part III (page 10).
- Build an ice house (page 16).
- Choose one or more of the Extending the Book activities (page 8).

Lesson 10

- Sequence main ideas to make a poster of the story (page 12).
- Complete one or more of the Extending the Book activities (page 8).
- Complete the Culminating Activities (pages 70-72).

Overview of Activities

SETTING THE STAGE

1. Prepare the classroom with a bulletin board for art and writing projects (page 75), a table with resource books about wolves from the library, and butcher paper for word lists.

2. Construct the research/activity center (page 74). Place the research forms (pages 54-56) in the center. Store art supplies in the center, too.

3. Display a map of Alaska to show students the setting of the story. Have students share any information they already know about Alaska.

4. Introduce students to the Eskimo way of life (pages 13-15).

Overview of Activities *(cont.)*

SETTING THE STAGE *(cont.)*

5. Before reading the story, have the students write a paragraph about all the information they already know about Alaska, the Arctic, Eskimos, wolves, or survival skills. Save their work. After students have finished reading the story, have them write about the same topic and add any new information they learned by reading the book. Then have students discuss the differences between the two paragraphs they wrote.

6. Tell students that this book deals with survival in the Arctic. Discuss other books or movies that describe survival in harsh conditions. Discuss the essential needs for survival: shelter, food, water, space, and companionship. On a piece of butcher paper, or on the overhead projector, have students brainstorm a list of skills and characteristics a person would need in order to survive in a harsh environment, such as the Arctic.

7. This story shows some different ways people and animals can communicate. Have students study how wolves communicate (page 60).

ENJOYING THE BOOK

1. Keep a class "diary" as you read the story. As you complete each part, have students brainstorm a list of the most important events. Write these on butcher paper. Be sure to have students include changes in the environment that signal the changing of the seasons. If you prefer, students can keep individual "diaries" to record the major events of the story.

2. Create an ongoing mural of the Arctic. Add pictures of any animals that are mentioned in the story.

3. Build a diorama that shows Miyax's makeshift house on the tundra, the wolf's den, or a scene from the book.

4. Miyax's pen pal in San Francisco was very important to the story. If possible, have students become a pen pal for students in another state or country.

5. In Part I, Miyax learned much from the wolves by observing them. List and discuss some of the observations she made and how they were important to her survival. Then observe an animal at home, in school, or at a park for a period of time. Record your observations and share them with the class.

6. In Part II, Miyax created a "color wheel" of memories, in which her different memories were related to colors. Create your own "color wheel" by writing down some memories from your childhood and relating them to colors.

7. Before reading Part III, ask students to predict what will happen next. Suggested questions: Will Miyax see the wolves again? Will Miyax survive and reach San Francisco?

8. In Part III, Miyax frequently saw the Northern Lights. Do some research about what the Northern Lights are and how they are formed. Use different art mediums, such as watercolors, chalk, pastels, crayons, etc., and create a picture of the Northern Lights. Then write a "found" poem (page 39) about the Northern Lights.

Overview of Activities *(cont.)*

EXTENDING THE BOOK

1. There are many comparisons made throughout the story. Have students make a comparison chart using one or more of the following topics: Miyax's life in the Arctic vs. Amy's life in San Francisco; Types of food Miyax found to eat vs. The foods you eat; Survival skills needed to survive in the Arctic vs. Survival skills needed in a large city.

2. Miyax needed other methods of telling direction besides using a compass. List some of the ways that Miyax determined direction. Do research to find out about other methods Native Americans and scouts use for locating directions and tracking. Prepare a demonstration or oral report for the classroom.

3. Have students look at the map of Alaska and see if they can determine what route Miyax was traveling. Have them draw or write some alternate routes Miyax could have traveled.

4. Ask students to brainstorm a list of examples describing how Miyax survived with and without the wolves' help. Ask students if she really needed the wolves for survival and who had a better chance of survival, Miyax or the wolves? Have them explain their answers.

5. The author uses many similes in her writing, such as, "Finally, she saw, like hundreds of huge black fingers, the antlers of the caribou beyond the turn of the horizon." Have students locate and illustrate other similes in the story.

6. In the story, Miyax creates songs and poems about the tundra and the wolves to keep herself from feeling lonely. Have students create a song or poem that would help them when they are feeling lonely.

7. January 24th is the day that the sun rises in the Arctic. Have students reread page 100. Ask them to make a watercolor scene (page 64) of this event.

8. The changing of the seasons was important to Miyax's survival. Have students brainstorm a list of the clues that Miyax used to determine that the seasons were changing. Then ask students what clues they use to tell the seasons are changing in their community.

9. Even in a large city, people need survival skills to be successful. Discuss what some of these skills might be. Have students present the information in the form of a pamphlet. Display the pamphlets.

10. In Part III, bounty hunting affects Miyax's life. Discuss how the Eskimos and Miyax felt about bounty hunting. Ask students to compare these attitudes to their own feelings. Have students draw an Arctic food web (pages 51-52). Discuss how the elimination of one part of the food web affects the other parts. Hold a class debate on the pros and cons of bounty hunting and its effects on wildlife.

11. Miyax mentions that nothing decomposes in the Arctic. Have students investigate this by conducting a science experiment on decomposition. Prepare two flower pots by placing equal-sized pieces of garbage, such as paper, plastic, foil, and food, in each. Then cover the items with an equal amount of soil. Put one flower pot in a warm place and the other in a freezer. After about three or four weeks, have students unearth the pieces of garbage and compare the rates of decomposition.

12. Have students rewrite the ending of the story.

Vocabulary Lists

On this page are vocabulary words that correspond to the three parts of the book. Vocabulary activity ideas can be found on page 42.

PART I

(pages 5-25)*	(pages 25-49)*	(pages 49-70)*
heave	gaunt	vaulted
discern	edible	incorrigible
tundra	buntings	foraging
snarl	regurgitated	crescendo
hibernating	tinder	cleaver
apologetically	shank	scoffing
lichen	knoll	diligently
quivering	seizes	reprimand
bayed	preened	menacingly
crooned	acute	quell
acutely	larvae	awed
barren	carrion	improvised
frigid	tawny	tribute
rigorous	torso	marveled
phenomenon	oblong	deft
mimicking	hamper	doomed
vitality	veered	obediently
gussaks	nomadic	predator
dispelled	conspicuous	splotched
pursuing	ruff	sinew
undulating		
ambrosia		

PART II

(pages 75-88)*	(pages 88-104)*
divinely	prosperous
kayak	upholstery
shaman	pinnacles
prancing	mythical
darted	clammy
dwelled	droned
metallic	Quonset hut
trough	foyer
crouched	eclipse
snickered	intricate
infinitely	irritated
taut	specks
soot	lapse
horizon	terminal
pried	tinker
canvas	reluctant
protest	convenience
ridiculous	dimension
sparklets	awesome
steep	crept

PART III

(pages 109-129)*			(pages 147-170)*	flourish
brandishing	lair	sputtering	artifacts	furred
groveled	cumbersome	barren	totem	constellation
niche	dome	flailing	grandeur	radiation
bravado	cauldron	constricted	abundant	magnetic
migration	roost	hypnotized	hoisted	treacherous
inquiry	immense	aurora	regal	harness
survival	thongs	simplicity	nestled	prosperous
deft	(pages 129-147)*	ferociously	avalanched	creased
elevated	maneuver	hibernation	tanned	annex
improvised	scheme	illuminated	pensions	resonant
bowed	massive	ravenously	yipping	
sauntered	ferocity	billowing	amber	
	bounty	veered		

Page numbers may vary slightly, depending on the edition of the book. Look for natural breaks in the reading to introduce the vocabulary words that are appropriate for the pages within that part of the book.

Discussion Questions

As you read the book, use these questions to generate discussion among students.

Part I

1. Miyax mentioned "two sleeps" and "many harpoon-shots away." To what was she referring?

2. Why did Miyax name the wolves? How did the names (Amaroq, Silver, Jello, Sister, and Kapu) match the personalities of the wolves?

3. Why did Miyax tie red cloths to the clumps of bushes? Why was it important for her to know which way was north?

4. How do the Eskimos define wealth? How does the Eskimos' definition of wealth compare to that of your culture?

5. What did Miyax keep in her pocket? What was its importance?

Part II

1. How are traditional and modern-day Eskimos similar? How are they different?

2. Miyax's father taught her, "When fear seizes, change what you are doing." What are some examples of when Miyax uses her father's advice? How could this lesson help you?

3. Miyax must deal with many strong feelings as her life changes. How do you think she felt during the following situations?
   A. When she discovered that her father was reported missing
   B. When she married Daniel and must live in a different house
   C. When she received Amy's letters

Part III

1. What problems arose between Miyax and the wolf, Jello? What was the result?

2. What was the most important to Miyax: her knife, matches and boots, or her food supply? Explain your answer.

3. In the story, Miyax dealt with many losses. How do you think these losses affected her response to the following situations?
   A. The bounty hunters and the death of Amaroq
   B. The change in her father as she remembered him
   C. The death of her bird, Tornait

4. Throughout the book, the main character is referred to by two names. What were these names, and what was the author's purpose for doing this?

Focusing on Language Arts

1. Write five adjectives from the story that describe the words "wolf" and "tundra."

Wolf	**Tundra**
_____	_____
_____	_____
_____	_____
_____	_____
_____	_____

2. Match these two columns to form compound words. Then on the back of this paper, use them in sentences related to the story.

sandpiper

sand — door
moose — piper
seal — place
wind — pack
ice — out
fire — skin
back — proof
out — song
hide — berg
sing — hide

_____
_____
_____
_____
_____
_____
_____
_____
_____

3. Fact and Opinion: *Fact = Miyax ate caribou meat. Opinion = Miyax loved to eat caribou meat.* Write two more facts and opinions, based on information from the story.

Fact: _____ Fact: _____

Opinion: _____ Option: _____

4. The word "kayak" is a palindrome, which means it is spelled the same whether you read it forward or backward. Write four more words that are also palindromes.

_____ _____ _____ _____

5. There are many Arctic animals mentioned in the book. Choose three of them and fill in the chart below, using the example given for "wolf."

animal	**word for their young**	**word for the group**
wolf	*pup*	*pack*
_____	_____	_____
_____	_____	_____

Sequencing Main Ideas

In this activity you will identify and sequence important events. You can choose to work alone or in a cooperative learning group.

Step 1:

After reading *Julie of the Wolves*, write down ten important events from the story.

Step 2:

Take a poster board, or a large piece of construction paper, and divide it into ten sections.

Step 3:

In each section, write a short paragraph describing one of the events. Make sure the events are written in random order on the poster.

Step 4:

Next, number the sections from one to ten, in any order you would like. Make an answer key that shows the correct order of events. Do not allow other students to see the answer key.

Step 5:

Display your poster in the classroom.
Place a small box or can underneath your poster.

Step 6:

Invite other students to examine your poster and guess what the sequence of events should be. Have them write their name and sequence of numbers on a piece of paper. Ask them to place their paper into the box or can. Remove the papers from the box or can and check the answers.

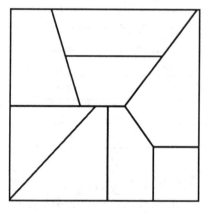

Step 2:

Step 3:

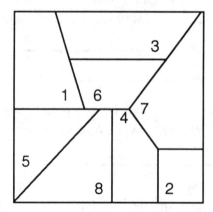

Step 4:

Answer Key: 8, 3, 7, 6, 4, 2, 5, 1

The Eskimo Way of Life

Eskimos are a distinct ethnic group who share the same ancestry and culture. Today, Eskimos blend the traditional way of life with the modern world. The word "Eskimo" comes from the Native American language meaning "eaters of raw meat." English explorers first used the word in the 1500's. Many Eskimos today prefer to be called Inuit, a word from their own language that means "the people."

Eskimos live in the Arctic region. Their settlements are scattered throughout Alaska, Canada, Greenland, and Siberia. The Arctic is actually a frozen, treeless tundra. It gets very little precipitation. In the winter, it is so cold that the snow does not melt. Deep snow covers the land. Oceans and bays are usually frozen by October. In most of the Arctic, there are few daylight hours. In the northernmost areas, the sun does not rise for months. In the summer, the tundra thaws for a short period of time allowing grasses, lichens, flowers, sedges, and shrubs to grow. For natural protection against the winds most of the plants are less than a foot high. There is nearly continuous daylight from the months May to September. The temperatures during these month can get quite warm— perfect for the thousands of mosquitoes. Shown below are some sample temperatures for the northernmost parts of the Arctic. Mark them on the thermometers in degrees Fahrenheit (^{0} F) or degrees Celsius (^{0} C). Then use the scales on the thermometer to determine the missing number. How do these temperatures compare to the ones in your area? You may wish to draw some thermometers on your own paper to record some local temperatures.

June 21: 36 ^{0} F or _____ ^{0} C
September 21: _____ ^{0} F or - 1 ^{0} C

December 21: _____ ^{0} F or - 18 ^{0} C
March 21: -9 ^{0} F or _____ ^{0} C

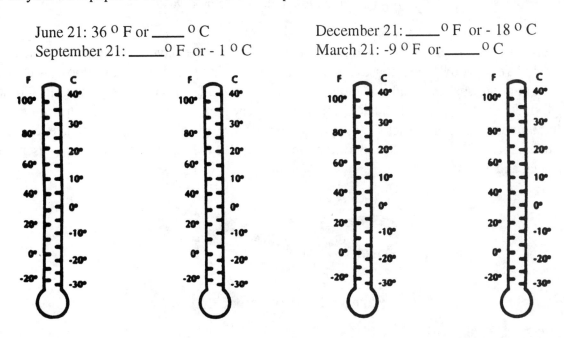

The Eskimo Way of Life (cont.)

The traditional way of life for the Eskimos included hunting, fishing, and trapping. They spent winters near the coasts where they could hunt seals and fish. In the summers, they would move inland to hunt caribou and gather berries. Cooperation among the members of the group was essential to their survival in this harsh land. Whales, crabs, many species of fish, walrus, lemmings and other small mammals, birds and eggs were all sources of food. Meat, fat, and fish made up a large part of the Eskimo diet because vegetables were scarce, and since the Eskimos used many different parts of the animals they hunted, very little went to waste. Listed below are some ways the Eskimos used the animal resources of the Arctic.

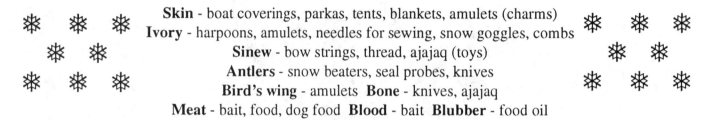

Skin - boat coverings, parkas, tents, blankets, amulets (charms)
Ivory - harpoons, amulets, needles for sewing, snow goggles, combs
Sinew - bow strings, thread, ajajaq (toys)
Antlers - snow beaters, seal probes, knives
Bird's wing - amulets   **Bone** - knives, ajajaq
Meat - bait, food, dog food   **Blood** - bait   **Blubber** - food oil

Eskimos are descendants of the Mongolian people of Siberia and share many of the same physical characteristics, including medium height; yellowish-brown skin; black, straight hair; and almond-shaped eyes. Scientists believe that the first Eskimos came to North America about 5,000 years ago by crossing the Bering Strait. The Eskimo language has been spoken for thousands of years, but it has not been written down until modern times. There are three main Eskimo languages. Inupik has the greatest number of speakers with only slight differences among dialects. Here are some examples of this language.

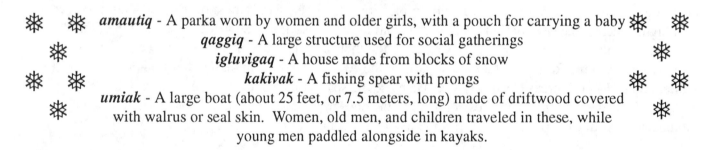

amautiq - A parka worn by women and older girls, with a pouch for carrying a baby
qaggiq - A large structure used for social gatherings
igluvigaq - A house made from blocks of snow
kakivak - A fishing spear with prongs
umiak - A large boat (about 25 feet, or 7.5 meters, long) made of driftwood covered with walrus or seal skin. Women, old men, and children traveled in these, while young men paddled alongside in kayaks.

Today Eskimos live with many modern conveniences. Snow mobiles have replaced sleds pulled by dogs. Most Eskimos live in wood-frame houses and apartments instead of ice houses, or igloos. Although many Eskimos still hunt on weekends and vacations, canned and frozen foods are widely used. In addition, factory-made products, such as parkas and television sets, are very popular. However, modern conveniences have brought modern problems, such as low-paying jobs, low levels of education, violence, crime, and alcoholism. Today, many Eskimos are trying to re-establish some of the old ways in order to preserve their culture, language, and crafts.

"Farewell, till we meet again."

The Eskimo Way of Life (cont.)

Locate and circle the following words in the wordsearch puzzle below.

ajajaq	amulets	Arctic	caribou	cooperation
culture	descendants	dialects	Eskimo	igloos
igluvigaq	Inuit	language	lemmings	lichens
parka	sinew	sled dogs	survival	tundra

```
S O M V B J J S X I B T U N D R A A Z M X X N
N T D N W Y M W Z P S T B L K L H Q G J J Y D
S M C F T U V R C W R K M H A S T E L U M A V
Q R B E Q I M E W X G W F N D Z J S S M R R J
V W V A L Z G K O Y G Z G B S C F P Y E U R O
C Y L Q V A Z X U A A U L K P E P O V U Z U H
E R K K F T I X Y P A A C X T Y E N E A I C L
A M C M L F A D W G K O S F J C I T C R A M S
X J R N A D T I E R O W K H T N C G E N L K S
F Y A T C W Y Q A P L E E W A N K J R E V T L
L G S J F U Q P E J Y S D E Z Y W R V K N N A
R E G I A R L R Z L M K B G L N I W S A L O V
M H M U S Q A T R J B I D L T L B V D Q G P I
S V H M O T X U U R P M O R R S P N L I J F V
I U T B I B E E V R E O G T S V E Y U F U H R
J T N O W N I Z N T E O S N X C A S W R I S U
M F N L Q U G R W A O N E P S M U I I X I O S
W T I U N I L S A V D H F E K F J N M C B O N
C Y L R D Q C W K C C Q D C F R I E U W I L H
C R H U T L X N H I D J Q R Y I B W V N R G X
V W P K V A A Q L T I A E Q A G I V U L G I U
S L E D D O G S Z I F L A S V K A N J J T K O
```

Now unscramble these words, using the list shown above.

1. nratdu -_____

2. msieok -_____

3. tiiun -_____

4. cictar -_____

5. rbacuio -_____

6. aakrp -_____

7. mnmeglis -_____

8. eulucrt -_____

9. onoaotcripe -_____

10. qijaaa -_____

Build an Ice House

In Part III, Miyax decided to live as the Eskimos did long ago, so she built herself an ice house. Today, most Eskimos live in modern wood-frame houses or apartments. But for many years, the ice house, or igloo, was the Eskimos' traditional home. It was used primarily as a temporary shelter when the Eskimos moved to new hunting grounds during the cold winter months.

An ice house takes about one or two hours to build. An Eskimo starts by drawing a circle in the snow. A long, sword-like knife is used to cut out blocks from the snow. Each block is about two feet (0.6 meters) long, 1 foot (0.3 meters) high, and 1 foot (0.3 meters) wide. The blocks are then laid along the circle that has been drawn in the snow. About six blocks are sliced and used to form a ramp. This is the key to forming the dome shape. More blocks are added until the dome is complete. Then the spaces between the blocks are filled with snow. An air hole is cut into the top of the dome. A larger square is usually removed to form a window. Finally, a hole is cut for the entrance, and a "porch" is added.

The inside of the ice house is kept warm using lamps. A low "couch" is made out of snow. It is used as a table during the day and covered with animal hides to make a bed at night. A block of snow provides an inside door, and wooden poles are used for hanging racks. The food supply, which consists of frozen fish and seal, is stacked alongside the wall.

Activity

Work with two or three other students or by yourself to build an "ice house." Use a large piece of cardboard as the base and draw a circle on it. (You may prefer to use Plexiglas or clear plastic as your base. This way you can add interior features and view them from the bottom by looking through the Plexiglas or plastic.) Use sugar cubes as your ice blocks. Be sure to plan your design before you glue your sugar cubes together. Glue the cubes together according to your plan. Allow the glue to dry. Then use a rough surface, such as a nail file or sandpaper, to round the edges of the cube to create the dome shape. Use additional glue to fill in any gaps between the cubes. Allow the glue to dry again, and add interior features if desired. (If sugar cubes are not available, the ice blocks can be made from white modeling clay. Use small bits of clay to fill in the gaps between blocks.)

The Call of the Wild

by Jack London

Summary

This adventure story describes the life of a dog named Buck. Buck is stolen from his home in Santa Clara, California, and sold by the gardener's helper because the man has heavy gambling losses. The dog is shipped north to Alaska where he is sold as a sled dog. Buck must learn the harsh lessons of survival during the Klondike Gold Rush of 1897. He is treated with cruelty and contempt until he meets John Thornton. Thornton saves Buck from yet another beating by his owner. A special bond develops between Thornton and Buck as they come to love and trust each other. But Buck does not entirely depend on Thornton, and sometimes runs with a wolf pack. At the end of the story, Thornton is killed and Buck permanently joins the pack of wolves.

This outline shown below is a suggested plan for using the various activities that are presented in this unit. You should adapt these ideas to fit your own classroom situation.

Sample Plan

Lesson 1

- Introduce Alaska during the Klondike Gold Rush (page 18, #1, 3, 4).
- Use one or more of the Setting the Stage activities (page 18).
- Present background information about the author, Jack London (page 23).
- Introduce the vocabulary list for Chapter 1 (page 21).
- Choose a vocabulary activity (page 42).

Lesson 2

- Read Chapter 1 in *The Call of the Wild*. Begin a class diary (page 19).
- Choose one or more of the, Enjoying the Book activities (page 19).
- Present background information about wolves (pages 47-49)
- Introduce the vocabulary list for Chapter 2 (page 21).
- Choose a vocabulary activity (page 42).

Lesson 3

- Read Chapter 2.

- Add new information to the class diary (page 19).
- Continue working on Enjoying the Book activities (page 19).
- Introduce the vocabulary list for Chapter 3 (page 21).
- Choose a vocabulary activity (page 42).

Lesson 4

- Read Chapter 3.
- Add new information to the class diary (page 19).
- Introduce the vocabulary list for Chapter 4 (page 21).
- Choose a vocabulary activity (page 42).

Lesson 5

- Read Chapter 4.
- Add new information to the class diary (page 19).
- Learn about habitats (pages 68-69).
- Introduce the vocabulary list for Chapter 5 (page 21).
- Choose a vocabulary activity (page 42).

Sample Plan *(cont.)*

Lesson 6

- Read Chapter 5.
- Add new information to the class diary (page 19).
- Continue working on Enjoying the Book activities (page 19).
- Introduce the vocabulary list for Chapter 6 (page 21).
- Choose a vocabulary activity (page 42).

Lesson 7

- Read Chapter 6.
- Add new information to the class diary (page 19).
- Solve some mathematics problems related to the story (page 25).
- Complete Enjoying the Book activities (page 19).

- Introduce the vocabulary list for Chapter 7 (page 21).
- Choose a vocabulary activity (page 42).

Lesson 8

- Read Chapter 7.
- Complete the class diary (page 19).
- Discuss the story (page 22).
- Begin working on newspaper stories (page 26).
- Choose one or more of the Extending the Book activities (pages 19 and 20).

Lesson 9

- Finish newspaper stories (page 26).
- Complete one or more of the Extending the Book activities (pages 19 and 20).
- Complete the Culminating Activities (pages 70-72).

Overview of Activities

SETTING THE STAGE

1. Prepare the classroom with a bulletin board for art and writing projects (page 75), a table with resource books about wolves and Alaska during the Klondike Gold Rush, and butcher paper for word lists.

2. Construct the research/activity center (page 74). Place the research forms (pages 54-56) in the center. Store art supplies in the center, too.

3. Display a map of North America (page 74). Discuss the settings for the story – Santa Clara Valley in California and Dawson in the Yukon Territory. Have students locate, mark, and label these two places on their map of North America (page 61). Ask students to share any information they already know about Alaska or the Klondike Gold Rush.

4. Before reading the story, have the students write a paragraph using all the information they already know about the Yukon Territory, sled dogs, Arctic life, or the Klondike Gold Rush. Save their work. After finishing reading the story, have them write about the same topic, adding any new information they have learned by reading the book. Discuss the differences between the two paragraphs that they wrote.

5. The main character, Buck, is a dog. He is given human traits and characteristics throughout the story. Giving human characteristics to animals and objects is called personification. Discuss other movies or books that include personification. Ask students why they think this is done in so many animal stories.

Overview of Activities *(cont.)*

SETTING THE STAGE *(cont.)*

6. Have students do research and present information about the Klondike Gold Rush in 1896. If possible, invite a gold prospector to speak to your class.

7. Introduce the author, Jack London, and his writing style by reading one of his other stories, such as "To Build a Fire." You may wish to show one of his stories that has been made into a video or movie, such as *White Fang.*

ENJOYING THE BOOK

1. Keep a class "diary" as you read the story. As you read each chapter, have students brainstorm a list of the most important events. Write these on butcher paper. If you prefer, students can keep individual "diaries" to record the major events of the story.

2. Obtain a large map of North America or enlarge the map shown on page 61. Help students use information from the story to draw in the route of Buck's journey. Have them label specific features, landforms, and cities that are along the route. Remind students that this is a fictional book, so there will be times when they must use their imagination to predict parts of the route.

3. Have students do research to find out what a Klondike mining camp looked like. Then have them create a three-dimensional display of a mining camp.

4. Before reading a chapter, have students read the title and predict what might happen next.

5. Have the class work together to create an ongoing time line. Vertically hang a piece of string or yarn. Using index cards, one for each chapter, estimate the length you will need. As the class completes a chapter, remove the next card and fold it in half. On one side, have a volunteer write about the most important event. On the other side, have a volunteer draw a picture about that event. Glue the card back onto the time line.

EXTENDING THE BOOK

1. Buck's life changed drastically from the beginning of the book. Make a comparison chart of his life in Judge Miller's home to his life in the Yukon Territory. Compare such things as: food, shelter, sleeping, working, climate, and morals.

2. Have students work in cooperative learning groups to examine how Buck's various owners treated him. Ask students to write down the name of each owner, and then list the positive and negative things Buck learned from each of them. Allow time for students to share their information with the class.

3. Have students choose one of the settings described in the story: Judge Miller's house, working as a sled dog in the Yukon, the attack by wild dogs at Lake Le Barge, the mining town of Skagway, or John Thornton's camp. Have them paint a scene or draw a detailed picture of one of these settings. Display students' work around the classroom.

Overview of Activities (cont.)

EXTENDING THE BOOK (cont.)

4. After students have completed the book, have them view a movie or video that has been made using this story. Ask students to list some of the similarities and differences between the book and the film. Discuss their lists.

5. Have students rewrite the ending of the story. Ask students: What could have happened if John Thornton had not been killed? or What could have happened if Judge Miller had found Buck?

6. Have students choose a section of the story that they enjoyed reading. Have them prepare to read the section aloud for the class. Remind them to practice the dialogues for expressive reading. Then have the class read their selections in chronological order. Make a tape to play back later.

7. Ask students to use craft sticks, toothpicks, and string to build a sled. They may wish to do some research to help them with this project.

8. Have students make a poster advertising the Klondike Gold Rush. The poster should encourage people to take their chance at looking for gold. Ask them to use the research from Setting the Stage, activity number 6, to create this poster.

9. Jack London uses descriptions and comparisons throughout the story to create a visual picture. Similes and metaphors are two types of comparisons London frequently uses. (A simile is a comparison that uses the words "like" or "as." A metaphor makes a comparison without using the words "like" or "as.") Divide the class into groups. Each group will need two people to record information. Have each group label two pieces of paper, one with the heading "Similes" and the other with the heading "Metaphors." Ask students to scan back through the story looking for similes and metaphors. Have one recorder write the similes and the other write the metaphors. Ask groups to compare their lists.

10. This story deals with survival. Have students create a board game in which survival in the Yukon Territory is the topic.

11. Have students work in groups or independently to write a sequel to the story: *The Son of Buck* or *Another Call of the Wild*.

12. Have students discuss how the title relates to the story. Have them locate the sections in which "the call" was first mentioned, and when they first got a hint of how the book might end.

13. Ask students to create a new book jacket. Tell them to be sure to include the title, the author's name, and the illustrator's name on the book jacket. Have them draw a scene from the story on the front, write a summary of the story on the inside front flap, write a biographical sketch of the author on the inside back flap, and write comments and quotes from people who have read the book on the back of the cover.

14. There are two major themes to the story. Choose one and write examples from the book that support that theme. Then write in your own words how that theme could relate to your environment.

   A. *Even the most civilized being has a primitive side.*
   B. *Those who are the most fit are the most likely to survive.*

Vocabulary Lists

On this page are vocabulary words that correspond to the chapters of the book. Vocabulary activities can be found on page 42.

Chapter 1
(pages 3-21)
groping
boughs
realm
treachery
deft
eloquently
wrath
ferocity
primitive
mediated
toil
domain
kindred
menacingly
lacerated
taunted
evelation
swarthy
culprit

Chapter 2
(pages 25-40)
peril
combatants
draught
flank
venom
arduous
apt
ravenous
malingerer
clamor
leeward
vicarious
comradely
gaunt
forlorn
courier
fastidious-
ness
mode
callous
cadences

Chapter 3
(pages 43-67)
dominant
prone
pandemoni-
um
trice
marauders
singed
bristling
cunning
mutiny
pall
bedlam
wraith
primordial
famished
daunted
shirked
nocturnal
solidarity
wan
rend

Chapter 4
(pages 71-86)
gaping
triumphantly
monotonous
friction
floundered
remnant
coveted
unruly
potent
morose
churned
perplexed
obdurate
thrashing
forevalued
loafing
solidarity
stoppages
mushers
half-breed

Chapter 5
(pages 89-114)
callowness
chaffering
dwindled
taut
repugnance
capsized
voracious
incompe-
tence
grievance
galvanized
idle
feigned
slovenly
forged
zeal
quaver
shorn
chivalrous
loom
wielded

Chapter 6
(pages 117-140)
ministra-
tions
vibrant
savor
chasm
jutted
impede
exploit
sheen
maneuver
momentum
expediency
shrewdly
tolerated
malicious
veered
capable
clamor
mysterious
pivoting
impulse

Chapter 7
(pages 143-172)
muck
melancholy
flintlock
tangible
commingled
formidable
fabled
shrouded
vague
lope
pent
defied
compelling
quest
obliterated
subdued
vigils
quarry
void
agility

Discussion Questions

As you read the book, use these questions to generate discussion among students.

1. How would you describe Buck's mother and father?

2. How would you describe Buck at the beginning of the story? How did he change by the end of the story? Do you think these changes were positive or negative? Explain your answer.

3. List two other animals from the story. How were they important to the events in the story?

4. What lesson did Buck learn from "the man in the red sweater"? Who were some of Buck's other owners and how did they treat him?

5. What were the "law of the club" and the "law of the fang"? How did these "laws" affect Buck's life?

6. How were the people in the Santa Clara Valley similar to those of the Klondike region? How were they different?

7. How would you describe the rivalry between Buck and Spitz? What were the results of this rivalry?

8. Buck often dreams about a hairy man. What do you think this dream symbolizes?

9. What qualities would a person need in order to be a good driver for a sled dog team and to survive in the Yukon? How can you tell that Charles and Mercedes have a poor chance of survival?

10. What makes John Thornton a good master for Buck? How does Buck change when he is away from Thornton in the wild?

11. How did John Thornton meet Buck?

12. What was the bet Thornton had with Matthewson?

13. Why do you think John Thornton was killed?

14. What was "the call of the wild"? How did this change Buck's life?

15. Why were the Yeehats afraid of Buck?

Jack London

Jack London, 1876-1916

Jack London's life was as rugged and filled with adventure as his stories. He was born in San Francisco, California, on January 12, 1876. He grew up around the docks of San Francisco and Oakland, developing a love for boats and the ocean. At the age of thirteen, he left school to help support his family. London was bored delivering papers and working in an Oakland factory, so he joined a band of men who illegally caught and sold oysters. By the age of 19, Jack London had become one of the most successful oyster pirates working in the San Francisco Bay area.

Throughout his life, Jack London maintained a strong love for books, but he led a wild life that took him from place to place and from job to job. He hunted seals, worked in a jute factory, and went to the University of California to study English. He traveled to Japan and the South Seas, and marched in Washington D.C. with socialists who wanted economic change and justice. When the Klondike Gold Rush started in 1897, London went prospecting for gold in Alaska. But he, like so many others, did not strike it rich.

When he returned from Alaska, he started writing short stories about life in the Yukon. He married Bess Maddern in 1900, and in the next few years they had two daughters, Joan and Bess. In 1903, while writing a short story about a dog, he could not stop. His imagination was strong and vivid. Within thirty days, he had created *The Call of the Wild*. It was soon bought by a publisher for 2,583 dollars. The book and Jack London became popular all over the United States, as well as the rest of world.

After this success, Jack London became a correspondent for a San Francisco newspaper. He covered the Russo-Japanese War in the Orient. People loved his exciting and colorful dispatches. One assignment led him to London, England where he lived in and wrote about the poorest slums in the city. He divorced his first wife, and married Charmain Kittredge. London spent his time traveling, sailing, and writing. His life was filled with action, as were his stories. In addition to *The Call of the Wild*, he also wrote *The Sea Wolf, The Iron Heel, The Valley of the Moon, White Fang,* and *The Cruise of the Snark*. Over a 17 year period he wrote fifty books and a large number of short stories. London, who was a heavy drinker, was burdened by debts and frequently criticized for his political views and writings. Pressures such as these may have led to London's taking an overdose of drugs, resulting in his death on November 22, 1916, in Sonoma County, California. London was 40 years old.

Jack London *(cont.)*

Use the clues shown below to fill in the word puzzle about Jack London.

1. _____ J __ __ __ __
2. __ __ __ __ __ __ __ A __ __ __ __ __ __ __
3. __ __ __ __ __ C __ __ __ __ __ __ __ __
4. __ __ __ __ __ __ __ K __ __ __ __ __ __ __ __

5. __ __ __ __ __ __ __ L __ __ __ __ __ __ __ __
6. __ __ __ __ __ __ O __ __ __ __ __ __ __
7. __ __ __ __ __ __ N __
8. __ __ __ __ __ D __ __ __
9. __ __ __ __ __ __ O __ __ __ __ __ __
10. __ __ __ __ __ __ __ N

Clues:

1. Jack London held many of these during his life
2. The city where London was born
3. This is the first name of London's second wife
4. The name of the 1897 gold rush
5. The title of London's book that became popular all over the world
6. The place where London was a correspondent for the Russo-Japanese War
7. The country London was living in when he wrote about slum conditions
8. What his death was caused by
9. The animals London illegally caught and sold in the San Francisco Bay area
10. London's age at the time he left school

Now do research to learn about the Klondike Gold Rush in which Jack London participated. Make your own word puzzle with information about the gold rush in the frame below.

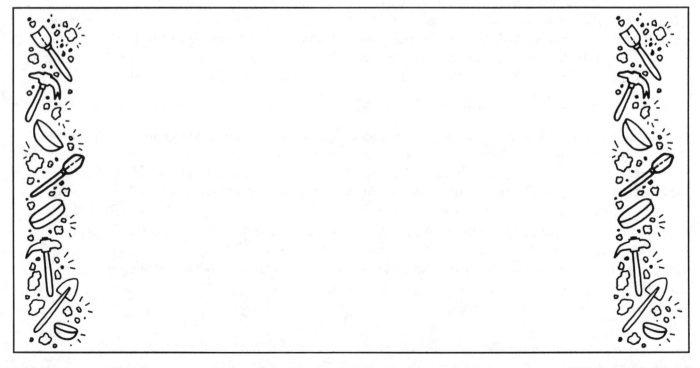

Mathematics in the Yukon

Adventure literature provides many opportunities to show students that math is needed as a daily living skill. Using quotes from *The Call of the Wild* have students use math skills to solve the following problems.

---

1. "The Thirty Mile River was wide open. Its wild water defied the frost, and it was in the eddies only and in the quiet places that the ice held at all. Six days of exhausting toil were required to cover those thirty terrible miles." (page 49)

   It is about 600 miles (966 km) from Dyea, Alaska, to Dawson in the Yukon Territory.
   A. If the sled team traveled 30 miles (48 km) per day, how long would it take them to reach Dawson?
   B. If the weather and the trail held up, the sled team could travel up to 50 miles (81 km) per day. Then how long would it take them to reach Dawson?

---

2. "It was a record run. Each day for fourteen days they had averaged forty miles. For three days Perrault and Francois threw chests up and down the main street of Skagway...." (page 77)
   A. How many miles did they cover in fourteen days?
   B. If they had traveled for three weeks and continued to average forty miles per day, how far would they have gone?
   C. If they wanted to cover the same distance in ten days that they had covered in fourteen, how many miles would they have needed to average per day?
   D. Perrault and Francois bragged for three days. How many minutes did they brag?

---

3. "Buck had sprung in on the instant; and at the end of three hundred yards, amid a mad swirl of water, he overhauled Thornton." (page 128)
   A. Buck swam 300 yards (270 m) to reach Thornton. How many feet was that?
   B. If Buck could swim one yard (0.9 m) in 5 seconds, how long would it take him to reach Thornton and swim back to shore?

---

4. "The crowd fell silent; only could be heard the voices of the gamblers vainly offering two to one. Everybody acknowledged Buck a magnificent animal, but twenty fifty-pound sacks of flour bulked too large...." (page 137)
   A. How much weight is twenty fifty-pound sacks of flours?
   B. If they were using ten-pound sacks of flour, how many sacks would they need to have the same amount of weight?
   C. The odds were two to one. If someone bet twenty dollars, how much money could that person win? How much money could that person lose?

Klondike News

In this activity students will develop higher-level thinking skills by summarizing story events using a newspaper format.

1. After reading *The Call of the Wild*, divide the class into cooperative learning groups. Each group will be responsible for producing a newspaper about the story. Give students a specific deadline for turning in their completed newspaper.

2. Have students examine various local and national newspapers. Discuss the layouts of the different sections. Students may wish to keep these newspapers for later reference.

3. Have group members select one of the following jobs:
   - Lead Story Reporter - writes facts about major events
   - Editorial Reporter - writes an opinion for or against a particular issue
   - Feature Writer - writes about the facts and historical aspects of an event
   - Sport Reporter - writes about sports-related events
   - Book Reviewer - writes a short summary and gives an opinion about the entire book

4. Have students brainstorm a list of possible story topics for their newspaper.

5. Provide each group with several large sheets of newsprint.

6. Now each group must make decisions about the following things.
   Layout of the Newspaper - where the stories, pictures, ads, etc. will be placed
   Article Titles - need to catch the reader's attention
   Fillers - includes information that can be used to fill any empty spaces

   Remind students that they will never see empty space in any real newspaper.
   Here are some suggestions for fillers:

• *Letters to the Editor*	• *Weather Maps*	• *Coming Attractions*
• *Comic Strips*	• *Advertisements*	• *Political Cartoons*
• *Classified Ads*	• *Puzzles*	• *Classified Advertisements*

7. Have students add any extra details to their finished newspapers. Have groups share their newspaper with the class. Have students discuss the positive things they liked about one another's newspapers. You can provide students with additional newspaper writing experiences by ordering a resource book with hands-on activities together with sets of 15 four-page, realistic newspapers (TCM 906, *Newspaper and Reporting Set*) from Teacher Created Materials, Inc.

Klondike
News
Jobs
Head Story
Reporter Bonnie

Kävik the Wolf Dog

by Walt Morey
Summary

Kävik, half wolf and half dog, is the lead dog for the winning sled team in a race called the North American Sled Dog Derby. His life takes a dramatic turn when he is sold to Mr. George C. Hunter. Hunter puts Kävik in a cage and places him aboard a small airplane bound for Seattle, Washington. After surviving the crash of the airplane, Kävik is nursed back to health by a young boy named Andy. This wonderful story describes the powerful friendship between a boy and a wolf-dog. It takes place in the wilderness of Alaska, and is a blend of adventure, suspense, and courage.

This outline is a suggested plan for using the various activities that are presented in the book. You should adapt these ideas to fit your classroom situation and the ability of your students.

Sample Plan

Lesson 1

- Introduce Alaska (page 28 #3).
- Present background information about wolves (pages 47-49).
- Use one or more of the Setting the Stage activities (pages 28-29).
- Introduce the vocabulary list for Chapters 1 and 2 (page 31).
- Choose a vocabulary activity (page 42).

Lesson 2

- Read Chapters 1 and 2 in *Kävik the Wolf Dog*.
- Begin a class diary (page 29 #1) Enjoying the Book
- Make a chart showing the adaptations of some arctic animals (page 36).
- Choose one or more of the Setting the Stage activities (pages 28-29).
- Introduce the vocabulary list for Chapters 3 and 4 (page 31).
- Choose a vocabulary activity (page 42).

Lesson 3

- Read Chapters 3 and 4.
- Add new information to the class diary (page 29).
- Learn about habitats (pages 68-69).
- Write a story about animal tracks (page 40).
- Use one or more of the Enjoying the Book activities (pages 29-30).
- Introduce the vocabulary list for Chapters 5 and 6 (page 31).
- Choose a vocabulary activity (page 42).

Lesson 4

- Read Chapters 5 and 6
- Add new information to the class diary (page 29).
- Use one or more of the Enjoying the Book activities (pages 29-30).
- Introduce the vocabulary list for Chapters 7 and 8 (page 31).
- Choose a vocabulary activity (page 42).

Sample Plan *(cont.)*

Lesson 5

- Read Chapters 7 and 8.
- Add new information to the class diary (page 29).
- Make a model of a wolf skull (page 67).
- Use one or more of the Enjoying the Book activities (pages 29-30).
- Introduce the vocabulary list for Chapters 9 and 10 (page 31).
- Choose a vocabulary activity (page 42).

Lesson 6

- Read Chapters 9 and 10.
- Add new information to the class diary (page 29).
- Create a family tree for wolves (pages 53-56).
- Use one or more of the Enjoying the Book activities (pages 29-30).
- Introduce the vocabulary list for Chapters 11 and 12 (page 31).
- Choose a vocabulary activity (page 42).

Lesson 7

- Read Chapters 11 and 12.
- Add new information to the class diary (page 29).

- Learn how to graph data (pages 57-58).
- Complete Enjoying the Book activities (pages 29-30).
- Introduce the vocabulary list for Chapter 13 (page 31).
- Choose a vocabulary activity (page 42).

Lesson 8

- Read Chapter 13.
- Complete the class diary (page 29).
- Discuss the story (page 32).
- Complete a crossword puzzle about the story (page 33).
- Choose one or more of the Extending the Book activities (page 30).

Lesson 9

- Sequence the main events of the story (page 34).
- Examine similarities and differences (page 44).
- Complete one or more of the Extending the Book activities (page 30).
- Complete the Culminating Activities (pages 70-72).

Overview of Activities

SETTING THE STAGE

1. Prepare the classroom with a bulletin board for art and writing projects (page 75), a table with resource books about wolves and Alaska, and butcher paper for word lists.

2. Construct the research/activity center (page 74). Place the research forms (pages 54-56) in the center. Store art supplies in the center, too.

3. Display a map of North America. Point out the setting of the story from Seattle, Washington, up through Alaska. Collect newspaper and magazine articles about Washington and Alaska. Display them around the map throughout the unit.

Overview of Activities *(cont.)*

SETTING THE STAGE *(cont.)*

4. Have students preview the book by looking at the title, the summary on the back of the book, and illustrations in the book. Ask students to write one or more paragraphs predicting what they think might happen in this story. Save these papers until students have finished reading the book. Then use the first activity for Extending the Book shown on page 30.

5. The salmon and cannery industry provides a livelihood for some of the characters in the book. Ask students to do research about the salmon industry. Have them identify some vocabulary that is pertinent to this field and investigate the environmental pros and cons, as well as the problems associated with seasonal work. If possible, invite a salmon fisher or a cannery representative to speak to your class. Have students have a debate to discuss the two sides of this environmental issue.

6. Tracking animals to hunt for them is described in this story. Kävik, also uses tracking to hunt for prey. Have students discuss tracking they have done. Have them research different animal tracks or invite a tracking expert to speak to the class. Ask them to write a story about animal tracks (page 40).

ENJOYING THE BOOK

1. Keep a class "diary" as you read the story. As you read each chapter, have students brainstorm a list of the most important events. Write these on butcher paper. If you prefer, students can keep individual "diaries" to record the major events of the story.

2. Keep a class timeline as you read through the book. You will need to tape a string along a wall in your classroom. As the class reads each chapter of the book, discuss what important events should be added to the timeline. Have volunteers use construction paper to draw a picture and write a short summary for each event. Then use clothespins, paper clips, or tape to attach the pieces of construction paper to the string with the events in sequential order.

3. Provide students with copies of the map of North America (page 61). Have students work in cooperative learning groups to use an atlas to locate and label Fairbanks, Alaska, where the story begins. Have students work with their group to mark the map with Kävik's approximate route as he travels from place to place. Have them label important cities and landmarks that are mentioned in the story. Remind students that this is a fictional book, so there will be times when they must use their imagination to determine Kävik's route. After students have finished reading the story, ask them to compare their maps.

4. Make a diorama of some important places described in the story. Some suggestions for dioramas include: Kävik winning the North American Sled Dog Race in Fairbanks, Alaska; the crash site; Andy's kitchen; Doctor Walker's office; George Hunter's house and yard; Martha and John's boat; the glaciers and tundra Kävik traveled across.

5. Have students find the word "vein" on pages 54 and 57. Discuss how this word is used in two different ways. Have students work in cooperative learning groups to locate other words in the story that have multiple meanings. Ask students to add to their list as they encounter new words while reading.

Overview of Activities *(cont.)*

ENJOYING THE BOOK *(cont.)*

6. On page 72, the author refers to the "rock in Andy's stomach." Ask students what this expression means. Have them brainstorm a list of other expressions that could be substituted for the one in the book.

7. The author describes the arrival of spring on page 72. Have students draw two pictures of what they think Copper City or Andy's home would look like in the winter and in the spring.

8. In Chapter 7, George Hunter is going to give a speech about Alaska, and he uses Kävik as a point of interest. Design a poster advertising the event.

9. Before students read Chapter 13, have them predict how the story will end.

EXTENDING THE BOOK

1. Have students write a summary of the book. At the beginning of the story, students wrote predictions about the story. Return those papers to students. Ask students to compare their two papers. Have them discuss which predictions were closest to the events in the actual story. Ask them to suggest reasons why some predictions were closer than others to the story events.

2. Show the video, *Kävik the Wolf Dog*. Have students discuss the similarities and differences between the book and the video. Ask students to suggest ways that the video or the book could be improved.

3. Have students write an epilogue to the story. Ask them to think about what Kävik's life would be like in one, five, or ten years from the time that the story ended. Have them predict whether Kävik and Andy will remain together and whether Kävik will ever become a sled dog racer again.

4. Have students write a journal through the eyes of one of Kävik's owners. Ask them to think of daily events about which a person might write.

5. Have students work in cooperative learning groups to make a Big Book of Kävik the Wolf Dog. Have them draw the major events on posterboard and bind them together. Then have them use the Big Book to tell Kävik's story to younger children.

6. Have students compare this story to other animal stories, such as *The Incredible Journey*. Ask them to make a chart showing similarities and differences.

7. Have students find passages or examples from the story in which the use of at least one of the five senses is described. On the chalkboard make a chart with the following headings: Sight, Hearing, Touch, Taste, and Smell. Have students list examples from the story on the chart. Then have them make a graph to show which sense was used most frequently.

8. Have students staple two file folders together to make a stand-up display. Ask them to decorate it with information about the book. Tell them to be sure to include the following: title, author, summary, illustrations, information about Alaska, a map of Alaska, objects or artwork related to the story. Obtain permission to allow students to set up their displays at the school or public library, other classrooms, or local businesses.

Vocabulary Lists

Chapters 1 and 2
(pages 11-29)
grueling
surged
oblivious
wary
confines
frenzy
mantle
ravenously
gorge
sate
deliberately
truce
bedlam
milling
tenders
rending
insecure
rending
strident
talons
feeble
flank

Chapters 3 and 4
(pages 30-50)
cannery
stealthily
gauging
eerie
convulsively
visualized
veterinary
gallant
ordeal
tundra
grotesque
harness
sliver
precious
barren
welled
surmises
nuisance
stethoscope

Chapters 5 and 6
(pages 51-85)
pallet
tenacity
anxiously
aroma
proffered
laboriously
seine
pursuit
fringe
punctured
grimy
dormant
morsel
deftly
scraggly
sheen
scrounged
hazards
eventual

Chapters 7 and 8
(pages 86-118)
palatial
acrid
intervals
savagely
oppressive
threshing
slunk
tang
awkward
peer
immense
circuit
plumed
grovels
tremendous
seething
veered
slaked
stealth
clamor

Chapters 9 and 10
(pages 119-148)
malamute
galley
plying
grub
sensitivity
stern
torrents
billowed
glade
jugular
galvanized
locale
reared
impassable
homing
hampered
disgorging
geysered
feint
vastness

Chapters 11 and 12
(pages 149-170)
frolicking
subter-
ranean
permeated
Chinook
unscalable
sapped
precarious
bounds
haunch
etched
crevasses
cache
fatigue
ravine
venison
rouse
harbingers
glacier
ptarmigan

Chapter 13
(pages 171-192)
wavered
pell-mell
emaciated
laboriously
vital
disintegrated
bored
specter
racked
defiant
timidity
bellow
curs
confined
jackknife
hobble
mongrels
cannery
ingloriously
deliberation

31

Discussion Questions

As you read the book, use these questions to generate discussion among the students.

1. Answer the five "W" questions about this story: Who, What, Where, When, and Why?

2. List five people and two animals from the story. Describe how these people and animals affected Kävik's life.

3. What kind of relationship did Kävik have with his first owner, Charlie One Eye?

4. What are some of the suspenseful situations in which the author makes you feel that Kävik will not survive?

5. When Andy first found Kävik, what did he intend to do? Why did Andy change his mind?

6. Why didn't Doc Walker want anyone to know he was treating Kävik?

7. How did Kävik's life with Andy's family differ from his life with Charlie One Eye? How did these differences influence the course of the story?

8. Why didn't Kävik make a full recovery in Chapter 6? Explain your answer.

9. When George Hunter takes Kävik, how does Andy feel? Do you think Andy's parents should have let him say good-bye to Kävik? Explain your answer.

10. How was Kävik's life different in Seattle? Did Kävik like it or not? Explain your answer.

11. In Chapter 8, why does Martha feel as if she has betrayed Kävik when she helps the men capture him? How does she change the situation?

12. Why did Kävik leave Martha and John when they docked? How would his life have been different if he had stayed with them?

13. In Chapters 10, 11, and 12, Kävik must survive in the wild. What are some examples of times when "wolf" qualities helped him survive? What are some examples of times when "dog" qualities helped him survive?

14. How did Kävik and Andy's father, Kurt, share characteristics of cowardice in Chapter 6? How did they share characteristics of bravery in Chapter 13?

15. What is your opinion of the story? If you could rewrite the story for the author, how would you change it?

Crossword Puzzle

Use words from the story to complete the crossword puzzle. The first one is done for you.

Across:

3. The cold, barren landscape of the North
5. An animal doctor
6. The area around a dog's back legs
9. Kävik was part dog and part _____
11. A type of fishing boat used in this story
12. A slow-moving iceberg on land
13. The type of fish used at the cannery
14. The area around a dog's mouth

Down:

1. The name of the animal Andy rescued
2. A small piece of wood
4. The sharp claws of a bird
7. A scent or smell
8. Deer meat
10. The type of skills you use to stay alive
15. The last name of the man who bought Kävik for $2000

Sequencing Main Ideas

In this activity you will work with three other students to identify and sequence important events from the story.

1. After reading *Kävik the Wolf Dog*, your group will be responsible for making a mobile that shows four main events from the story.

2. First, have your group choose four important events from the story. Have each group member choose one of the events.

3. Second, have your group gather the following supplies:
    four 12 inch by 12 inch (30 cm by 30 cm) squares of construction paper in any color
    scissors
    glue
    crayons, markers, or colored pencils
    paper scraps
    string or yarn

4. Now follow these steps for each of the four squares.
    Step 1: Fold the square from corner to corner two times so that the folds make four triangles.
    Step 2: Cut a slit from one corner to the center of the square.
    Step 3: Overlap the two triangles that are next to the slit so that a three-dimensional triangle is formed.

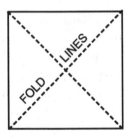 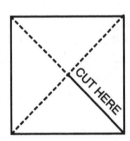 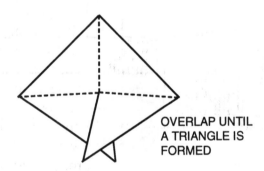

OVERLAP UNTIL A TRIANGLE IS FORMED

5. On one side of each triangle, have a group member draw or use paper scraps to illustrate the chosen event. Then glue a written summary of the event to the bottom face of the triangle.

6. Glue the four finished triangles together with the events in sequential order to create a pyramid. After the glue dries, tie a piece of string or yarn through the top of the triangle cluster. Then hang the mobile from the ceiling.

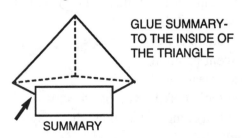

GLUE SUMMARY TO THE INSIDE OF THE TRIANGLE

SUMMARY

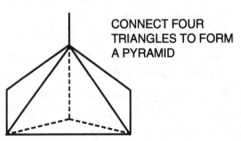

CONNECT FOUR TRIANGLES TO FORM A PYRAMID

Arctic Animals

To survive in the harsh tundra environment, Arctic animals must develop special physical traits called adaptations. Through the years of evolution, each type of animal has developed its own ways of coping with its environment. Here are some interesting facts and information about some of the many animals that live in the Arctic.

Lemming

The lemming is a very small herbivore, which means it eats only plants. It is grayish-brown in the summer, and changes to white in the winter. This camouflage helps it to hide from predators. This mammal's thick, waterproof fur helps to keep it warm. Strangely, every three or four years the lemming population greatly increases. This trend toward population growth can cause drastic events to occur, such as a large number of lemmings suddenly running off cliffs. As a result of these drastic events, the lemming population rapidly decreases over the next three or four years.

Caribou

The caribou is a large, light brown herbivore. It migrates throughout the Arctic searching for food. Its short tail and small ears help it to conserve heat. It has the widest feet of all the deer, to help it run across the snow. The caribou is also called the reindeer. Sometimes thousands of caribou travel together in a herd.

Polar Bear

The polar bear is a very large animal and can weigh up to 1,700 lbs (771 kg). It is an omnivore that eats mostly meat along with some plants. Its fur is yellowish-white in the summer, and turns to pure white in the winter. This coloring helps the polar bear blend in with its surroundings. The thick, furry hair on its feet provides warmth and works like snowshoes. It has webbed feet so it can swim easily. This mammal eats large amounts of food in the autumn in order to produce the fat it needs for warmth and stored energy to survive the winter. Since the polar bear does not hibernate, it builds a den in the snow or rocks to protect itself from the cold while it rests.

Walrus

The walrus is a carnivore, which means it eats only meat. It is very large and can be gray or cinnamon colored. Its skin has a thin fur coat and a thick layer of fat, or blubber, underneath it to help provide warmth. The walrus with the largest ivory tusks has the greatest status in the community. The tusks are used for weapons and as ice choppers. The walrus has sensitive whiskers that help it search for food in the darkness at the bottom of the ocean.

Narwhal

The narwhal is a large bluish-gray sea mammal. It is a carnivore and migrates to search for food and avoid frozen waters in the Arctic. This animal is virtually waterproof because of the oil glands in its skin.

Arctic Animals *(cont.)*

Ptarmigan

The ptarmigan is a medium-sized bird that usually eats plants but sometimes eats meat, making it an omnivore. Its feathers provide camouflage since they are mostly brown in the summer and white in the winter. The feathers on its feet provide extra warmth and help it shuffle through the snow. This bird spends most of its time on the ground. During the winter it will burrow into snowbanks for warmth.

Snow Goose

The snow goose is a large bird that is a herbivore. It comes in two colors — all white or dark gray with a white head. The snow goose has a large number of feathers to trap air for better insulation. In the autumn, this bird consumes large amounts of food to produce a heavy layer of fat so it will have enough energy to migrate south in the winter. Sometimes you will see a snow goose with a white body and an orange head. This occurs when a bird eats large quantities of plants from Arctic waters. These plants are high in iron content, causing the bird's head feathers to turn orange.

Activity

Make a chart similar to the one below to show how adaptations help the animals described on pages 35-36.

ANIMAL	ADAPTATION	PURPOSE OF ADAPTATION
Lemming		
Caribou		
Polar Bear		
Walrus		
Narwhal		
Ptarmigan		
Snow Goose		

Haiku Poetry

Haiku poetry originated in Japan. The Japanese people have a great appreciation for beauty and nature. Japanese poets write haiku to celebrate their love of the world around them. Here are two examples of haiku.

A tree frog blinking
As raindrops begin to fall
New life is around.

A pond shimmering
The sun shines brightly on it
In the early dawn.

What is Haiku?

Haiku consists of three unrhymed lines. Each line has a specific number of syllables, or beats. The first line contains five syllables and sometimes tells where the poem takes place. The second line contains seven syllables and sometimes tells what is happening in the poem. The third line contains five syllables and sometimes tells when the poem takes place.

How to Write Haiku?

Follow these steps with the entire class or in small groups. Use the chalkboard, overhead projector, or butcher paper to record students' ideas. If you prefer, students can keep their own record of ideas on notebook paper.

Step 1: Find some haiku poetry in the library to read aloud as examples. Suggested books include: *A Few Flies and I* by Yayu Issa, and *In a Spring Garden* by Richard Lewis.

Step 2: To practice, select an object from nature or a photograph of a scene to stimulate ideas. Discuss the object or scene with the class and record their ideas. For example, you could show students a picture of some wolves.

Step 3: Have students brainstorm a list of words or phrases that tell **Where** the action occurs.
      Examples: *the edge of the woods*   *on the Arctic landscape*   *among the trees*

Step 4: Have students brainstorm a list of phrases that tell **What** happens.
      Examples: *wolves howling at the moon*   *wolf pups singing for joy*   *wild dogs baying*

Step 5: Have students brainstorm a list of phrases that tell **When** the action occurs.
      Examples: *at the strike of midnight*   *before the rising of the sun*   *after the hunt*

Step 6: Have students pick one phrase from each of Steps 3, 4, and 5, and write them together.
      Example: *the edge of the woods*   (from Step 3)
                    wolves howling at the moon   (from Step 4)
                    after the hunt   (from Step 5)

Step 7: Adjust the syllables and words to fit the haiku pattern.
      Example: *The edge of the woods*   *(5 syllables)*
                    Wolves howling at the full moon   *(7 syllables)*
                    After the big hunt.   *(5 syllables)*

Step 8: Now, have students write and illustrate their own haiku poetry using the frames on page 38.

Haiku Poetry *(Cont.)*

Write and illustrate two haiku about wolves in the boxes shown below.

"Found" Poems

A "found" poem is a piece of writing that was not intended as a poem, but rewritten and declared poetry by its "finder." Newspaper and magazine articles or books can be used to create "found" poetry. Read the following article about the red wolf.

"The red wolf is a predator and must hunt other animals for food. Its favorite prey includes rodents, rabbits, raccoons, deer, and wild pigs. However, due to a loss of habitat, the red wolf must sometimes look for new sources of food. Livestock, chickens, and turkeys can become the wolf's new prey. As a result, many ranchers have a strong dislike for the wolf. These ranchers are against reintroducing the red wolf into wilderness areas."

Here is a "found" poem about the red wolf based on the article shown above.

predator
food, prey
loss, habitat
dislike, ranchers
reintroduce, wilderness
Wolves.

Here are the directions for how to write a "found" poem. You can work on this activity by yourself or with two or three other students.

Step 1: Choose a topic, such as Arctic Animals. (Look at pages 35-36 for the names of some Arctic animals. You can even use the information on these pages to create your "found" poem.)

Step 2: Choose a source of information for your poem. Sources can include: newspaper articles, magazine articles, reference books, or other nonfiction books. You might find the source of your information in your classroom, in your school library, at home, or in your community.

Step 3: After you have chosen your source of information, read it carefully. Write a list of the words and phrases that catch your attention or help to create a mental picture about the animal.

Step 4: Organize the words you have written on your list into a poem. You may wish to use all of your words or only some of them. You can also add any extra words you need.

Animal Tracks

Most of the time, you rarely see animals in the wild. That is because most animals will quickly take cover when people come near, and some animals are active only at night. However, you can often find evidence that animals have been around by looking at the tracks they leave behind. By studying these tracks, you can often figure out what these animals were doing, where they were going, what they preyed upon, and what preyed upon them. Here are some tracks and the names of the animals that make them.

Paws or Hooves?

The shape of the track can tell you if it was made by an animal with paws or hooves. Some pawed animals, such as foxes, walk on their "tiptoes," so only the center pads and toes on their feet show. Animals with hooves, like horses, cows, and elk, are also "tiptoe" walkers. Other animals, such as raccoons, walk flat-footed, forming a print of their whole paw.

Claws?

Small triangular marks in front of paws are made by claws. Coyotes, foxes, and dogs often leave claw marks. But most cats, such as cougars and lynx, leave no claw marks. This is because they sheathe their claws when they walk or run.

Speed? Direction?

The patterns of tracks will change from singular or parallel to diagonal as animals change their gait. In mammals that bound, such as rabbits, the hind feet will appear before their front feet. Look for claw marks or pushed up snow or soil to see which direction an animal is traveling.

Activity

On a separate sheet of paper show an event by drawing animal tracks. Then write a story to tell about what happened to the animals who left the tracks.

"The Boy Who Cried Wolf"

You have probably heard or read the story about the shepherd who tricked the villagers into coming to his rescue by crying, "Wolf!" In the story, the young shepherd is watching his family's flock of sheep in a pasture. It was a boring job so the boy decided he would cause some excitement. He ran from the pasture and yelled as loudly as he could, "Wolf! Wolf!" All of the villagers left their homes to save the boy and his flock. However, when they arrived at the pasture, they found there was no wolf, only a laughing shepherd and his flock. The shepherd had so much fun, he decided to try this trick again and again. Each time the villagers would come to his rescue, and each time the boy would only laugh at them. Then one day a wolf really did enter the pasture. Now the shepherd really did need help! He yelled with all of his strength, "Wolf! Wolf!" But no one came to his rescue.

Use the space below to rewrite the story of "The Boy Who Cried Wolf" from the wolf's point of view. You may wish to add some illustrations to your story.

_____

_____

_____

_____

_____

_____

_____

_____

Ideas for the Vocabulary Lists

1. Use the vocabulary words as weekly spelling lists.

2. Have students find the vocabulary words in the story. Copy the sentences from the story that contain vocabulary words. Rewrite the sentences using synonyms, or write your own sentences using the words the same way as the author.

3. Have students make word puzzles. Give students graph paper to make their own wordsearch or crossword puzzles using the vocabulary words. Have them trade with a partner and solve each other's puzzle.

4. Divide the class into groups. Assign a list of words to each group. Have each group be responsible for creating a game using their word list. Examples: Bingo, Wheel of Fortune, Jeopardy, Spelling Bee. Have the class play the games the groups have created.

5. Have students categorize the words into groups.
    Examples: • *nouns, verbs, adjectives, adverbs, etc.*
                       • *spelling rules from your spelling book*
                       • *prefixes, suffixes, and root words*

6. Have students alphabetize each list of words.

7. Using a newspaper, have students cut out the letters to form the words from the list. See how many words students can make in twenty minutes. Have them make a class collage of the words they glue together.

8. Have students use the words to write sentences, stories, or poems.

9. Have students play a definition relay. Divide the class into teams. Each member of a team must look up a vocabulary word and write its definition, then pass the list on to another member of the same team. Allow students to continue working until the end of a time designated by you. At the end of the time limit, have the teams exchange word lists. Ask students to check each other's definitions. The team with the most correct definitions wins the relay. You can vary this game by calling time when all of the members of one team have written a definition.

10. Have students practice their typing skills on a computer or typewriter using the vocabulary lists.

11. Have students work in cooperative learning groups to create an illustrated dictionary using the vocabulary words.

12. Have students play a form of concentration with their vocabulary words. The goal of this game is to have students match the vocabulary words with their definitions. Divide the class into small groups. Have students make two sets of cards that are the same size and color. On one set of cards, have them write the vocabulary words. On the other set of cards, have them write the definitions. All of the cards are mixed together and placed face down on the table or floor. A player picks two cards. If the pair matches the definition with the word, the player keeps the cards and takes another turn. If the pair doesn't match, the cards are returned face down to their places and the next player takes a turn. It is important for players to remember the locations of the words and their definitions. Students should continue to play until all of the matches have been made.

Wolf Sentences

This language arts activity is designed to help students write more interesting sentences and help reinforce their understanding of parts of speech. The finished sentences can then be used to write poetry, make big books, create illustrations, used for sentence dictation, or displayed on a wall or bulletin board.

1. Each student needs a piece of lined paper divided into four sections to make a chart with the following headings: Nouns, Verbs, Adjectives, Adverbs. Under the headings, each section should be numbered from 1 to 10. If necessary, draw an example on the chalkboard to show students what their chart should look like. Then review the four parts of speech shown on the chart. Ask students to brainstorm some ideas about the topic, "Wolves."

2. For the next ten minutes, have students write down a word under the heading for one of the parts of speech and exchange papers with a nearby student. Have them continue to write words and exchange papers with each other as quickly as possible. You may wish to have students exchange papers by pass ing them down rows or around in small groups. Remind students that each person can only add one new word to the chart before passing it on to another student. Words are not allowed to be repeated. After the ten minutes is up, return the charts to their original owners.

3. Next have students edit their paper. They may delete any words that are incorrectly placed on the chart. They may use a dictionary if they are not sure whether a word is written under the correct heading.

4. Review the words that students have written. Ask students to determine what was the greatest number of words listed under any one part of speech and what was the fewest number.

5. Then have the class work together to create sentences using the words students have written on their charts. Have them take one or more words from each category to form the sentences, adding any extra words that are necessary. Write these on the chalkboard as examples. Then have the students write their own sentences using the words from their chart. Have volunteers read their sentences to the class. Example: Many gray wolves howled at the moon after tracking their prey. You can help students learn to elabo rate by varying the above activity. Using the chart shown students can practice giving specific details and descriptions. Follow the same directions as are listed for the parts of speech activity.

Describing Words	Did What?
Where?	When?

    43

Examining Similarities and Differences

Think about the main animal characters that you read about: Amaroq in *Julie of the Wolves*, Buck in *The Call of the Wild*, and Kävik in *Kävik the Wolf Dog*. How are they similar? How are they different? Use the diagram below to show the similarities and differences among these three characters.

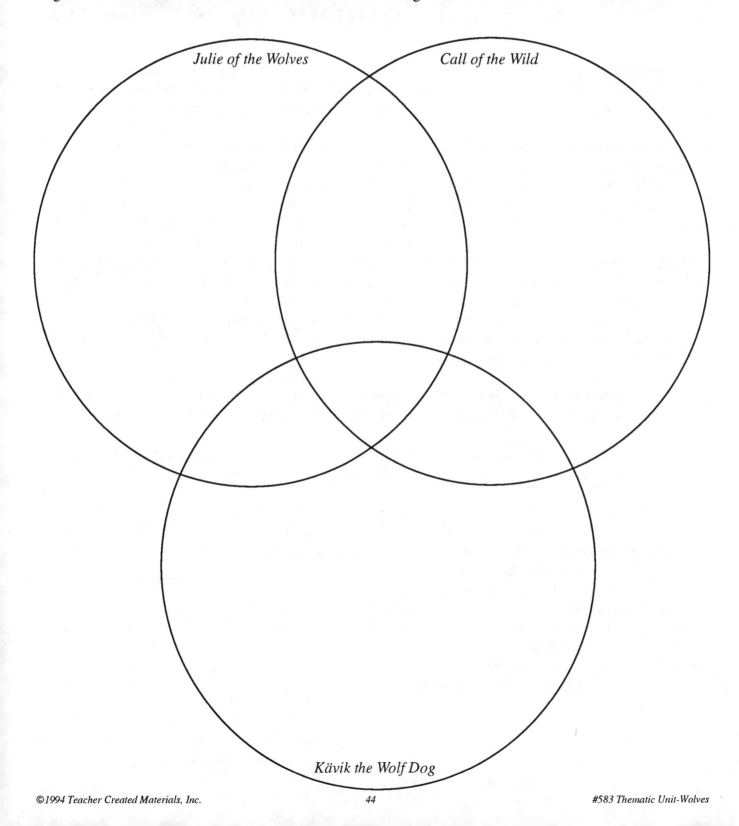

Letter Writing

Writing a letter is a good way to communicate. Here are two assignments for letters you can write. Use the letter-writing tips shown on page 46 to help you with these assignments.

Assignment #1:

The books you are reading describe how people are still hunting for wolves from airplanes. Write a letter to a government official stating your opinion and explaining the reasons for your opinion. You may wish to do some research about this topic so you can include this information in your letter.

Addresses:

The Honorable *(senator's name)*
U.S. Senate
Washington, D.C. 20510

The Honorable *(representative's name)*
U.S. House of Representatives
Washington, D.C. 20515

Assignment #2:

Many animals, like the wolf, are or have been threatened with extinction. You can find out more about different types of animals that are considered threatened or endangered species. Write a letter requesting information about a specific species in which you are interested. Send the letter to one of the organizations listed below.

Addresses:

Office of Endangered Species
U.S. Fish and Wildlife Service
Washington, D.C. 20240

Center for Action on Endangered Species
175 W. Main Street
Ayer, MA 01432

World Wildlife Fund
Suite 800
1601 Connecticut Ave., NW
Washington, D.C. 20009

National Wildlife Federation
1412 16th Street, NW
Washington, D.C. 20036

You can also write a letter if you are interested in finding out about threatened or endangered species that live in your area. Ask for information at your state's conservation department, parks and wildlife agency, natural resources department, chamber of commerce, or capital building. You might wish to call first to see which agency best meets your information needs.

Letter Writing Tips

Remember to...

1. Make your letter simple and direct. Research your topic, so that you are informed and can use facts to support your opinions.

2. Write about one problem or one request at a time.

3. Organize your ideas. First, state the reason you are writing. Then express your opinions and concerns. Conclude with any realistic suggestions you have for solving the problem. If you are requesting information, conclude with a polite request for the specific type of information you would like to receive. Be sure to include your address in the letter, so the person you are writing to can respond.

4. If possible, type your letter. If it is not possible, use your best handwriting so your letter will be neat and easy to read.

5. Before mailing your letter, check it thoroughly for errors in spelling, punctuation, capitalization, and grammar. Reread it to be sure it makes sense and is well organized. Have a friend or relative check over it, too. Then rewrite your letter and make any corrections that are needed.

6. Sign your full name (first and last) at the bottom of the letter. If you are asking for information, include a self-addressed envelope with two first-class stamps on it. Sending a self-addressed stamped envelope (SASE) increases your chances of getting a response.

7. Be patient while waiting for an answer. You can expect to wait three to six weeks for a reply. Make the most of any information you receive by sharing it with your class.

Follow this format when writing your letter.

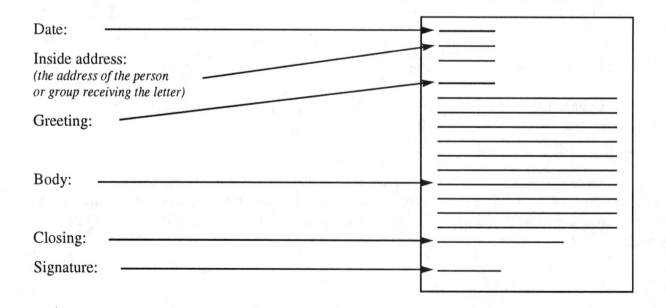

The Life of A Wolf

One of the most misunderstood animals of modern time, the wolf (canis lupis), is more illusive than deadly. The wolf has been feared since the time of westward movement across the United States. Myths about wolves have been perpetuated from the time of early childhood. Stories like "The Three Little Pigs" and "Little Red Riding Hood" help to strengthen these negative attitudes toward the wolf. Believed to be the killer of livestock and people, there has never been an actual documented case of a healthy, wild wolf killing a person in North America. Through education and understanding of the wolf, there will still be hope for its survival.

The Habitat

Historically the wolf roamed over most of Asia, Europe, and North America, having one of the largest natural ranges of any animal. Today the wolf is confined to small areas of wilderness. Depending on the species of wolf, it may be found in a variety of habitats, from deserts to plains and from seashores to mountains. As is the case with most other declines in animal populations, the loss of habitat is at the forefront. As the populations of people worldwide grew, more forests needed to be cut down, lessening wolf habitat. But, this was not the only cause of wolf decline worldwide. Other causes included hunting, poisoning, and trapping. Examine the map of North America. The shaded areas show where the range of the grey wolf (canis lupis) is today. Today the wolf is endangered, with fewer than 53,000 in existence. Why do you think there are more grey wolves found in Alaska than any other of the fifty states?

To learn more about the habitat of wolves, use the activities on pages 61 and 68.

The Body

In making a comparison, wolves look similar to large German shepherds. A full grown male wolf will weigh somewhere between 75-120 lbs. (34-54 kg), measure approximately 5-6.5 ft. (1.5-2 m) long, and stand about 2.5' (75 cm) off the ground. Female wolves are smaller. All of the wolf's senses are excellent, but three stand out above the rest. Its sense of sight, smell, and hearing allow it to locate prey easily. Wolves can smell and see prey from one mile (1.6 km) away. The wolf has 42 teeth and a strong jaw that enables it to hold onto, kill, and eat its prey. The long pointed teeth, called canines, are used for grabbing and holding prey. The teeth in the jaw, called carnassial, are used for crushing and slicing; and, the small teeth, called incisors, are used for picking meat off the bones.

The Life of A Wolf *(cont.)*

Wolves genetically adapt to where they live. For example, wolves that live in cold climates have short ears to help retain heat. Wolves that live in warm climates have long ears to release excess heat. The wolves two layers of fur protect them from their cold climates. The underfur is short, soft, and thick. This is protected by a top layer of fur consisting of long guard hair that keeps the underfur dry. Why do you think it is important for the underfur to stay dry?

Communication

Wolves "talk" to each other through a variety of sounds, such as growls, whines, yelps, and barks. They also use a variety of body movements. Some examples of wolf communication are listed below:

Play — Two front legs are extended, hindquarters raised, tail wagging, ears up, with an open-mouthed "grin." Even adult wolves like to play.

Greeting — When the leader returns, the wolves will gather around him and lick his muzzle to show recognition.

Warning — When a strange wolf enters a wolf pack's territory. Their fur will raise, ears move up and forward, head lowered, eyes stare, lips are raised, and teeth bared.

Scent marking — Wolves mark their territories by urinating on rocks, trees, etc. One sniff of a marked tree will tell a wolf if this is its territory or if it is trespassing.

Howling — It may occur during the day or night. It allows pack members to locate each other, may serve as an alarm or warning, and sometimes is done just for fun.

Look at page 60 to learn more about wolf communication.

The Life Cycle

Wolves are mammals and give birth to live pups. A female wolf may give birth to as few as one or as many as 11 pups, depending on habitat conditions. Wolf pups weigh 1 lb (.5 kg) at birth and are blind and deaf. They will live off their mother's milk for three weeks and then are able to eat meat. At this time they also leave the den for short periods of time. At two months they will leave the den for good and enter the hierarchy of the pack, where they are raised by all the wolves. At two years they are ready to mate for life. Why is it important for the whole pack to help raise the pups?
Use page 50 to make a life-cycle diagram for wolves.

The Pack

Wolves form into groups called packs. The wolves in the pack will live, hunt, and play together. A pack is made up of a male and female, their pups, and other relatives. The size can be from 5-30 wolves. There is a rank that exists within the pack and the communication discussed above is used so the wolves will not hurt each other. The leader, or alpha wolf, is usually the strongest wolf in the pack and will remain the alpha until challenged by a stronger wolf. The winner remains or becomes the new alpha, and the loser leaves the pack and becomes a loner. What benefits do wolves get by being part of a pack?

The Life of a Wolf (cont.)

Write **True** or **False** to answer these questions.

_____1. Gray wolves can be found in the southern part of the United States.
_____2. A wolf's sense of smell is much keener than a person's.
_____3. Wolves mark their territory by leaving scratch marks on trees.
_____4. A female wolf can have six puppies.
_____5. The omega wolf is the strongest member of the pack.
_____6. Incisors help the wolf pick meat off the bones.
_____7. Howling only occurs at night.
_____8. Wolves will mate for life.
_____9. Wolves are usually solitary animals.
_____10. Wolves will always attack herds of sheep.

Find these words in the wordsearch:

habitat

canis lupis

prey

underfur

howling

hierarchy

territory

alpha

endangered

Alaska

canines

yelps

dens

pack

mammal

wolf

```
S O M V B J J S X I B T W O L F A L P H A X N
N H A B I T A T Z P S T B L K L H Q G J J Y D
S M C F T U V R C W R K M H A S T E L U M A V
Q R B E Q I M E W X G W F N D Z J S S M R R L
V W V A L A S K A Y G Z G B S C F P Y E U R O
C Y L Q V A A X U A A U L K P E P O V U Z U H
E N D A N G E R E D Y A C X T Y E N E A I C L
A M C M L F I D W R K O S F J C I R C R L M S
X J R N A D S I O R O W K H T N C G E N A K S
F Y A T C W L T A P L E E W A N K J R E M T K
L G S J F U I P E J Y S D E N S W R V K M N A
R E G I A R P R Z L M K B G L N I W S R A O V
M H M U R Q I T R J B I D L T L B V U Q M P I
S V H E O T S U U S P M O K R S P F L I J F V
E U T B I B E E V P E O G C S V R Y U F U H R
N T N O W N I Z N L E O S A X E A S W R I S G
I F N L Q U G R W E O N E P D M U I I X I O N
N H I E R A R C H Y D H F N K F J N M C B O I
A Y L R D Q C W K C C Q U C F R I E U W I L L
C R H U T L X N H I D J Q R Y I B Q V N R G W
V W P K V A A Q L T I A E Q A G I V U L G I O
P R E Y M C A N I S L U P I S K A N J J T K H
```

Life Cycle Diagram

Make a life cycle diagram for the wolf. Do research to find out about the different stages of a wolf's life. You may also wish to use the information presented in "The Life of a Wolf" on pages 47-49. Use illustrations and sentences to tell about each part of the life cycle.

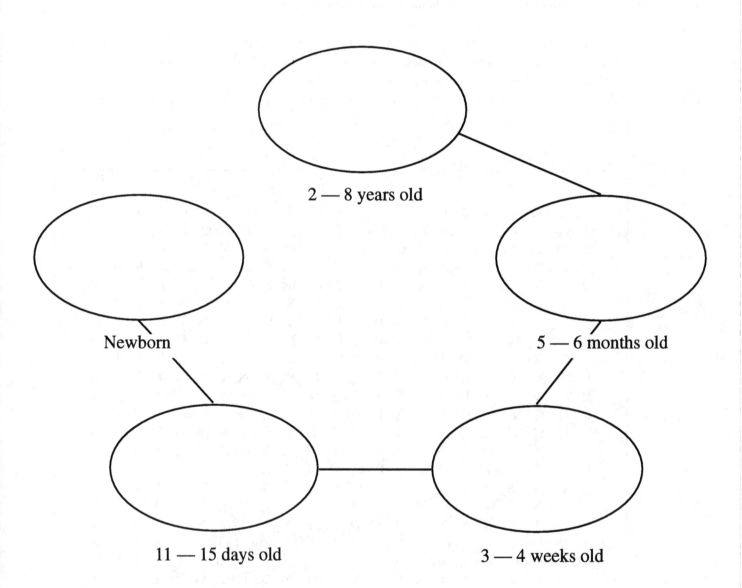

2 — 8 years old

Newborn

5 — 6 months old

11 — 15 days old

3 — 4 weeks old

Arctic Food Web

Living things need food in order to survive. A food chain shows how living things need each other for food. A green plant is usually found at the bottom of a food chain. The plant uses energy from the sun to carry on a process called photosynthesis. This allows the plant to produce its own food. As a result, the plant in a food chain is called a producer.

The producer, or plant, is eaten by an animal that is a herbivore, which is an animal that eats only plants, or an omnivore, which is an animal that eats plants and other animals. On the food chain, the animal that eats the producer is called a consumer. This is because it consumes the producer.

In the next part of a food chain, the consumer is eaten either by an omnivore or by another animal called a carnivore, which is an animal that eats only meat. This animal is also called a consumer.

Here is an example of a food chain. Notice that the arrows start with the producer and point toward the consumers.

Producer (Grass) → Consumer (Grasshopper) → Consumer (Bird)

There are many food chains living in a community. Some are very simple, while others are more complex. Since most animals eat more than one type of food, they might have several different food chains that can be made. When food chains connect or overlap, it is called a food web. If one part of the food web becomes extinct, the entire web may be affected, causing drastic consequences.

Here is an example of a food web:

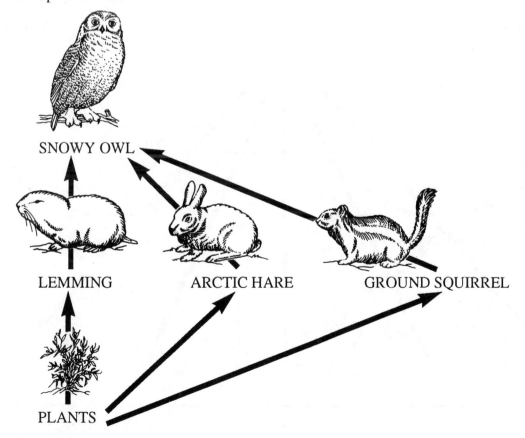

SNOWY OWL

LEMMING   ARCTIC HARE   GROUND SQUIRREL

PLANTS

The Arctic Food Web *(cont.)*

Use page 51 to learn about food chains and food webs. Then do the activity on this page. Do research to find out what kinds of things a wolf eats. Write down at least five of them. Some of the things a wolf eats are other animals. Research further to find out what those animals eat. Then use the space below to develop a food web using this information. Here is an example of a food chain that you can include as part of your food web: A wolf eats an Arctic squirrel which eats nuts and other plants.

WOLF

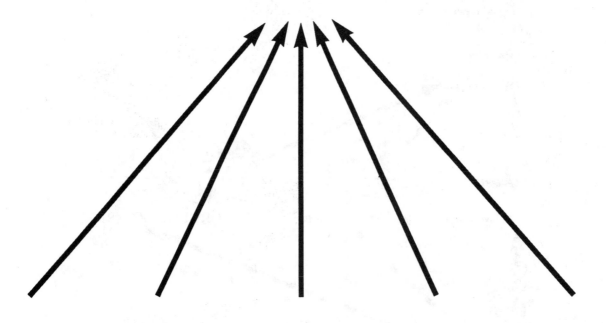

A Family Tree

Wolves, coyotes, jackals, foxes, and other species make up the family "Canidae," or dog-like mammals. Different species range all over the world and in every type of habitat. They vary in size from huge Arctic wolves to small fennec foxes. Throughout history, many people have feared wild dogs. Today, however, people are beginning to realize that wild dogs, such as wolves, are an important part of the food chain. They help to control the destructive rodent population. In addition, when game animals become too plentiful, wild dogs hunt and kill many animals that might otherwise starve to death. But has the appreciation for wild dogs come too late to help save some of the species that are endangered?

Work in cooperative learning groups to do research about wolves and other wild dogs. Some types of wild dogs are listed below. You may choose one of these to research or use a reference book to identify another group of wild dogs that is not listed on this page. Take notes using the form on page 54. Use the world map on page 55 to show where your wild dog lives. Use your notes to write a rough draft of your report on notebook paper. Then use the form on page 56 for your final draft. Hang your final draft and your map on the family tree bulletin board.

Wolves
      Gray Wolf
      Red Wolf
      Maned Wolf

Foxes
      Arctic Fox
      Fennec Fox
      Gray Fox
      Red Fox
      Bat-eared Fox
      Patagonian Fox
      Kit Fox
      Swift Fox
      Chama or Silver-backed Fox

Wild Dogs
      Coyote
      Coydog
      Bush Dog
      Dingoes
      African Wild Dog
      Raccoon Dog
      Azara's Dog
      Dhole
      Black-backed Jackal
      Silver-backed Jackal

A Family Tree *(cont.)*

Work in a cooperative learning group to do research about a type of wild dog. Use these forms to organize the notes that you take.

NAME OF WILD DOG:

Size: _____

Color: _____

Habitat: _____

Food Source: _____

Interesting Facts: _____

Sketch

NAME OF WILD DOG:

Size: _____

Color: _____

Habitat: _____

Food Source: _____

Interesting Facts: _____

Sketch

A Family Tree *(cont.)*

Mark and label the places on the map where your type of wild dog lives.

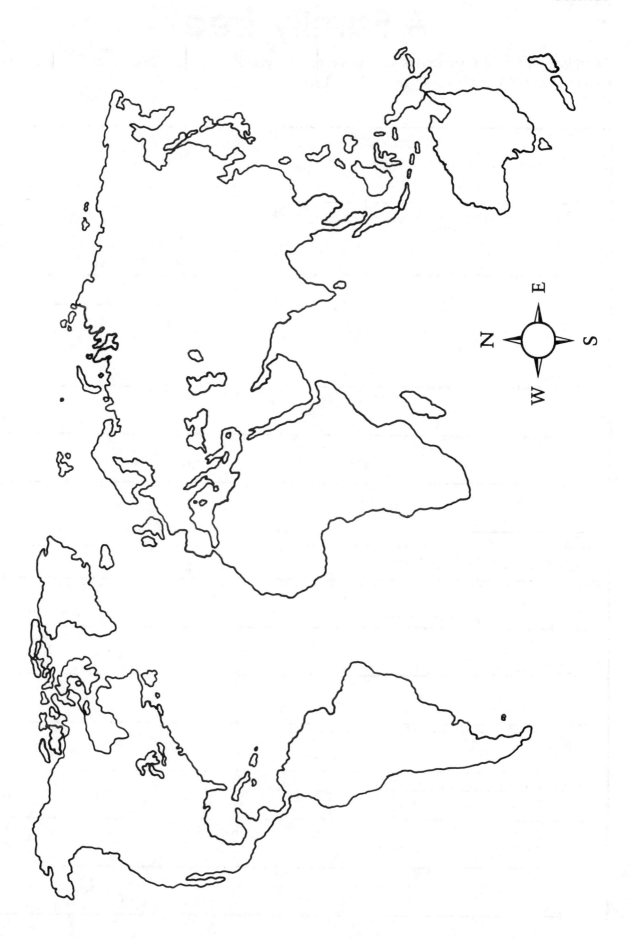

A Family Tree (cont.)

Use this form for the final draft of your report on one type of wild dogs. Place your final draft and your map from page 55 on the family tree bulletin board.

_____

Title

_____

By

_____

_____

_____

_____

_____

_____

_____

_____

_____

_____

_____

Graphing Activities

Make graphs to show the information recorded in each chart. Colors can be used to help you make comparisons.

1. On the graph, show the low weight and the high weight for each type of wild dog listed in the chart.

Adult Animals	Lowest Weights	Highest Weights
Gray Wolf	55 lbs.	155 lbs.
Coyote	25 lbs.	50 lbs.
Red Fox	8 lbs.	15 lbs.
Fennec Fox	2 lbs.	4 lbs.
Dingo	25 lbs.	50 lbs.

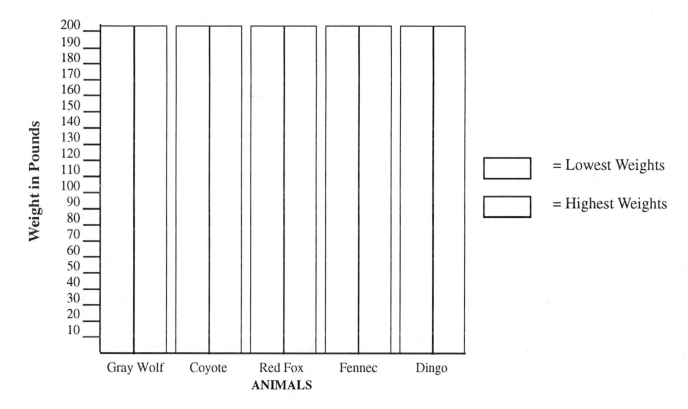

2. Use this chart to make two line graphs about body length and tail size.
   Draw your own grids for the graphs.

ANIMAL	BODY	TAIL
Gray Wolf	4 feet	15 in.
Dingo	5 feet	13 3/4 in
Coyotte	35 1/2 in.	13 1/2 in.
Red Fox	24 in.	17 in.
Fennec Fox	16 in.	7 3/4 in.

Graphing Activities *(Cont.)*

3. Use the information in the chart to make a bar graph showing the speed of wolves in comparison to other animals.

Animal	Speed mph.	Speed kph.
Wolves	40 mph.	64 kph.
Bats	15 mph.	24 kph.
Owl	40 mph.	64 kph.
Snake	2 mph.	4 kph.
Cheeta	70 mph.	110 kph.
Person	20 mph.	32 kph.
Goldfish	4 mph.	6 kph.

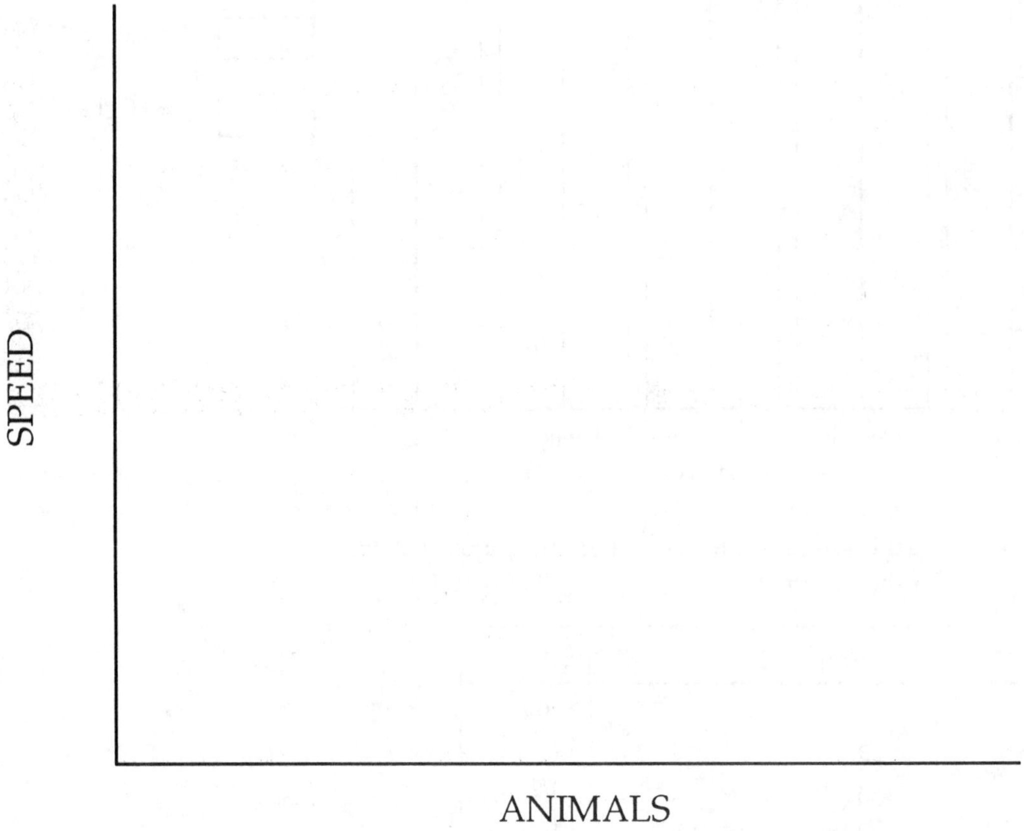

SPEED

ANIMALS

Inuit Ice Cream Recipes

Real Agutak Ice Cream

1 cup (236 mL.) caribou tallow, moose fat, or beef suet, melted
1 cup (236 mL.) oo-guk (seal) oil
1/2 cup (118 mL.) of water or snow
3 cups (708 mL.) crowberries or cranberries
3 cups (708 mL.) blueberries

1. Pour small amount of oo-guk oil slowly into the melted fat, whipping at the same time with your hands.
2. Add some water and continue to whip.
3. Whip in the rest of the oil and water, a little at a time, until the mixture becomes white and fluffy.
4. Stir in the berries.

Modified Agutak Ice Cream

2 egg whites
1/2 cup (118 mL.) vegetable oil, butter, or margarine
1 can tuna fish
2 tablespoons (30 mL.) vanilla
brown sugar or honey to taste
berries (optional)

1. Separate the egg whites from yolks. Beat the egg whites with a beater until stiff and fluffy.
2. In another bowl, put in the oil, and then spoon in egg whites a little at a time, and mix.
3. Add vanilla and brown sugar (or honey) to desired taste.
4. Mix in tuna fish.
5. Add berries, if desired. Makes enough for about two servings.

Activity

Pretend that you are having company and you want to double the recipes shown above. Use metric measurements and rewrite both recipes so you will have twice as much ice cream.

CONVERTING TO METRIC	
1 cup is approximately equal to	250 mL
1 oz is approximately equal to	25 g
1 lb. is approximately equal to	450 g
2.2 lbs is approximately equal to	1 kg
1 tsp. is approximately equal to	5 mL
1 T is approximately equal to	15 mL

Wolf Communication

Wolves are able to communicate many things, using their faces, bodies, and tails. Look at the illustrations that show how wolves communicate. Discuss how they communicate using body language. Try sending messages of your own to classmates using body language.

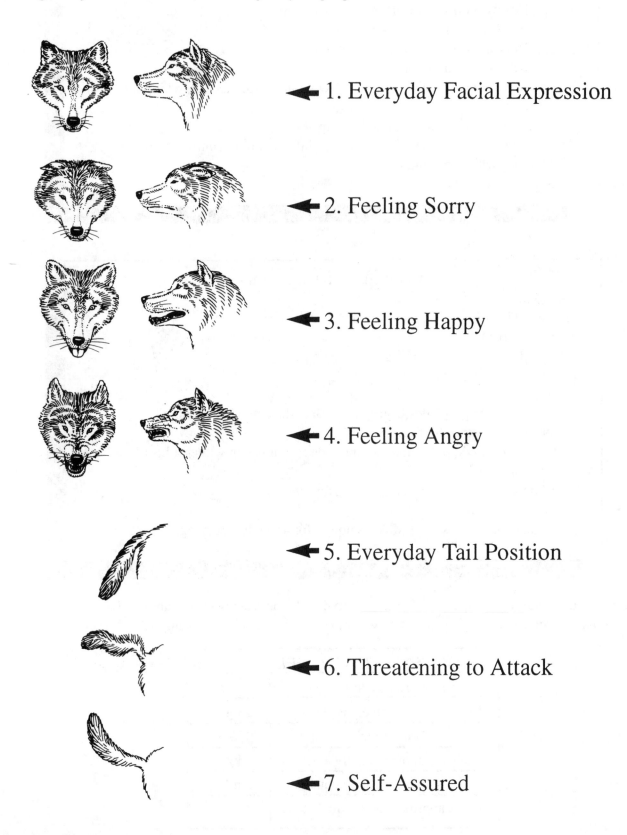

← 1. Everyday Facial Expression

← 2. Feeling Sorry

← 3. Feeling Happy

← 4. Feeling Angry

← 5. Everyday Tail Position

← 6. Threatening to Attack

← 7. Self-Assured

Wolves in North America

Look at the shaded area on the map. It shows where wolves in North America live. Learn more about where wolves live in North America by labeling the following places on the map.

Canada	United States of America	Mexico	Alaska
Great Lakes	Pacific Ocean	Atlantic Ocean	Hudson Bay
Greenland	British Columbia	Alberta	Saskatchewan
Manitoba	Ontario	Quebec	Labrador
New Brunswick	Nova Scotia	Yukon Territory	Northwest Territories

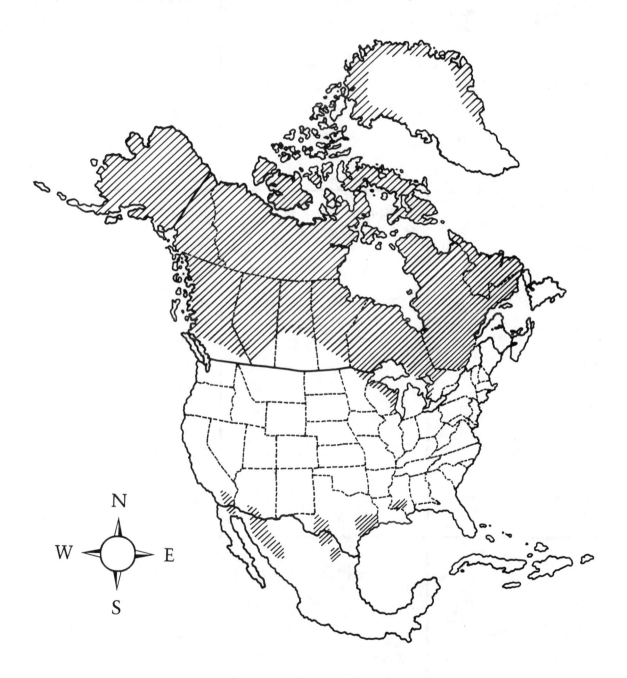

 Area where wolves live

Wolves: Fiction vs. Reality

Think about the facts you have learned by studying about wolves. Then remember how you usually see wolves characterized in stories, poems, movies, and cartoons. Use the diagram below to compare and contrast real wolves to their fictional counterparts. Some characteristics are shared by both realistic and fictional wolves.

You may wish to use the information about wolves found on pages 47-49 to help you recall specific facts.

Reality

"Wolves do not attack humans."

Fiction

"Wolves look very similar to dogs."

"Wolves regularly attack and eat people."

Wolf Masks

Native Americans have always respected wolves. Examine the three illustrations of wolf masks made by Native Americans. Use cardboard, papier–mache, construction paper, or another type of material to make one of these masks. Use paints, fabric, tissue paper, or construction paper to decorate the masks.

This type of mask is called a Wolf Crest and was made by the Kwakiutl. The mask has black eyes and eyebrows with blue and white markings around the eyes. Red is used around the nose and mouth, as well as above the eyes.

This is another type of wolf mask that was made by the Kwakiutl. The area around the eyes was blue and white. The top of the head, nose, and lips were red. The skull at the top of the mask was white.

This type of wolf mask was made by the Nootka. It was primarily blue, but the lips, designs, and top of the head were red.

Art

Watercolor Scenes

Materials:

    watercolor paints
    watercolor brushes
    black paper for silhouettes
    containers for water
    paper towels
    white construction paper
    newspapers for covering desks
    scissors
    glue
    optional — wolf outline pictures

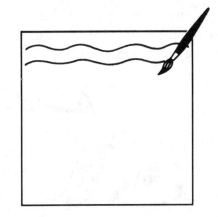 

Directions:

1. Cover the desks with newspapers. Pour water into containers until they are about half-full. Fold a paper towel in half for blotting the paint. Set out watercolor paints. Soften your paints by squeezing two or three drops of water into each color.

2. Plan the color "family" you are going to use. Some suggestions are listed in the box below. Choose three or four similar colors for a "family." Remember you can use the paint tray to mix your own colors. Try some of these combinations.

    warm colors (reds, oranges, and yellows)
    cool colors (blues and greens)
    try blending two colors like purples and pinks
    the colors of a sunset or midnight sky

Tip: Black, brown, and other very dark colors do not work well for silhouettes.

3. Wet a paper towel and squeeze out about half of the excess water. Then, use the paper towel to wash your white paper with water. Be sure to wipe horizontally across your paper. Next, dip your paintbrush into the paint and make brush strokes horizontally across the paper. Rinse your brush and change colors as frequently as you like. The paint will "spread" on the wet paper blending together with the next color. Continue making brush strokes across the entire paper with the paints in your color "family." If the colors are not "spreading" as much as you would like, wipe more water across the paper with your paper towel. If you want more color, add more paint to your brush and go over that area. If you have too much water on your paper, blot it with a dry paper towel. After your paper is filled with blended colors, allow it to dry. Clean up the watercolors and your desk.

4. Using black construction paper, cut out the figure of a wolf and other figures or shapes that you would like to use in your silhouette. When your watercolors have dried, glue on your figures and shapes. Trim off any overlapping pieces. If your picture has not dried flat, place some heavy books on top of it overnight. Display your finished watercolor scene.

Animal Magnets

In this activity, you will make animal magnets. To begin, you will need to prepare the craft dough. The materials and directions for preparing the craft dough are shown below.

Craft Dough

Materials:

> 4 cups (0.96 L) baking soda
> 2 cups (0.48 L) cornstarch
> 2 1/2 (0.5 L) cups cold water
> medium-sized saucepan
> spoon
> plate
> damp cloth
> plastic bag or plastic wrap

Directions:

Step 1: Be sure to follow all kitchen safety rules, and have an adult supervise as you make your craft dough.

Step 2: Place all the ingredients in a medium-sized saucepan and mix together using a spoon.

Step 3: Cook over a medium heat, stirring constantly.

Step 4: Cook for about 10 minutes or until the mixture is the consistency of mashed potatoes.

Step 5: Remove the pan from the heat.

Step 6: Use a spoon to push the mixture out of the pan and onto a plate.

Step 7: Cover with a damp cloth.

Step 8: After the dough has cooled enough to touch, gently knead into a smooth ball.

Step 9: Place it in a plastic bag or wrap it tightly in plastic wrap.

Step 10: Then, store the dough in the refrigerator until you need it for the magnets. This recipe should make enough dough for about 20 magnets.

Now you are ready to make your magnets. Decide which Arctic animals you would like to make. You can use one or more of the Arctic animals described on pages 35 - 36, or you can do research to get some ideas. After you have chosen the animals you want, draw sketches of them so you will remember what they look like. Then follow the directions on page 66 to make the magnets.

Animal Magnets *(cont.)*

In this activity, you will make animal magnets. First, you will need to prepare the craft dough as described on page 65. One batch will make about 20 magnets. Be sure to store the craft dough in a plastic bag and put in a refrigerator until you are ready to use it. Then, follow the directions shown below to make your magnets.

Materials:

> craft dough
> wax paper, to cover work area
> acrylic paints, watercolors, or markers
> clear nail polish, or acrylic sealer
> > (available at craft stores)
> small paintbrushes
> glue
> small magnets, or a magnet strip that can be cut
> > (available in craft stores)

Directions:

Step 1: Decide which Arctic animals you would like to make. Draw some sketches of the animals so you can refer to them as you make your magnets.

Step 2: Wash your hands before you begin to work with the dough.

Step 3: Place a piece of wax paper on your desk or work area.

Step 4: Take the craft dough out of the refrigerator.

Step 5: Flatten a golf-ball size lump of dough on the wax paper, using the palm of your hand.

Step 6: Press the dough until it is about 1/4 inch thick.

Step 7: Mold the dough into the shape of the animals, using your sketches as a guide.
Tip: It is usually easiest to mold the dough into the shape of an animal's head.

Step 8: Get another small lump of dough. Use tiny bits of this dough to make features, such as the eyes, nose, mouth, and spots.
Tip: Avoid adding features that are going stick out away from the animal, such as long, thin tails, horns, legs, etc. since these will easily break when the dough dries.

Step 9: You may wish to use a pencil point to carve in additional features.

Step 10: Let the dough dry overnight on the wax paper.

Step 11: The next day, remove the dried animals from the wax paper.

Step 12: Using acrylic paints, watercolors, markers, or all three, paint or color your animals. You can use realistic colors, or wild, imaginary colors. Let them dry.

Step 13: When the dough is dry, add a coat of clear nail polish or acrylic sealer to the animals. This will help protect your creations and make them shine.

Step 14: Glue a small magnet onto the back of each animal. If you do not have small magnets, cut small pieces from a magnet strip to make some. Then glue one of these onto the back of each animal.
Tip: Some larger animals may need two magnets.

Step 15: Let the glue dry thoroughly before using your magnets.

Wolf Skull Models

These diagrams show you how a wolf skull looks from the front and from the side. Examine these diagrams to see how the skull fits together. Then use clay or plaster to make a model of a wolf skull.

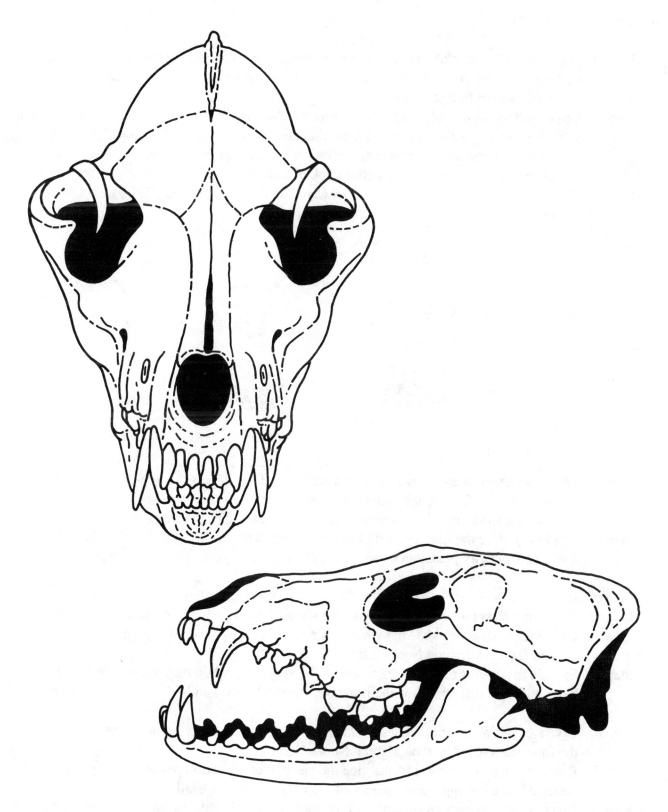

67

Life Skills

Understanding Habitats

In this activity, students will identify that an animal's habitat includes food, water, shelter, and enough space in which to live comfortably. Students will recognize that animals and people share the same basic needs.

Preparing for the Activity

Step 1: Draw an outline map of your school on the top part of page 69. Be sure to include the buildings and the grounds. Reproduce the map so that you can provide a copy to every group of three or four students.

Step 2: Draw wolf tracks on each map to show where a pack of wolves has gone. Each map should show tracks that go a different route, but that always begin and end at your classroom. (Safety Tip: Have the routes you create utilize a particular part of the school building and/or grounds so you can keep better track of students.

Step 3: Reproduce copies of the "Habitat Needs Card" on the bottom of page 69 so that every group will have one.

Step 4: Obtain some green and brown construction paper. Cut squares that are 2 inches by 2 inches (5 cm by 5 cm). Cut enough squares so that you will have four squares for each group. On each square write one of the habitat needs: food, water, shelter, enough space.

Step 5: Randomly place the squares around the routes you have marked. (Tip: Warn other teachers about your activity preparations so they will not pick up your construction-paper squares.)

Using the Activity

Step 1: Divide the class into cooperative learning groups consisting of three or four students.

Step 2: Give each team a map showing where it's pack of wolves have gone in the habitat. Then give each team a Habitat Needs Card.

Step 3: Explain to students that zoologists have to be very quiet when they study animals. Then have students begin to follow the route of their wolf pack as it is shown by the tracks on the map.

Step 4: Give students about ten minutes to find four construction-paper squares, one with each of the four needs listed on their Habitat Needs Card.

Step 5: Return to class and have students glue the piece of construction paper that they have collected onto the appropriate places of their Habitat Needs Card.

Step 6: Discuss the activity with students. Point out that animals must be able to get all of the things they need, when they need them, from the area in which they live.

Understanding Habitats *(cont.)*

Draw a map of your school here. Be sure to include the buildings, as well as the grounds.

WOLF HABITAT NEEDS CARD
These are the things a wolf needs in its habitat in order to survive.

Food

Water

Shelter

Enough Space

Write Your Own Wolf Adventure Story

Follow these steps to write your own story.

1. Get a piece of lined paper, and divide it into the following five sections:

	Who? — Main character: Name and describe your wolf. Supporting characters: These can include people and animals. Use words to describe your characters.
	When? — Describe the time period in which the story takes place. Use historical details to establish the time period.
	Where? — Describe the place or places where story events take place. You may wish to name specific physical landmarks or geographic features.
	What? — Make a list of events that you would like to happen in the order they should occur.
	Why? — Explain why your wolf is where it is at that time and why certain events occur.

2. First take some quiet thinking time to imagine your story. Then write information in the categories listed above. Next, look over each category carefully, filling in missing information, new ideas, etc. Tell a friend, teacher, or parent your ideas. Ask for suggestions on how to improve your ideas. List any ideas you wish to add. Do you have enough adventure, suspense, mystery and excitement to keep a reader interested?

3. Now take all your ideas and start writing paragraphs. This is a rough draft, so don't worry about such things as grammar, spelling, capitalization, and punctuation. Just write down your flow of ideas. Be sure to include plenty of details, have a logical sequence, build suspense, solve a problem, and conclude the story.

4. Re-read your story. Make any changes you feel are necessary. Now re-read your story again, editing it as you go. Use the Editing Checklist on pages 71 and 72 for help.

5. Decide what kind of book you want to make. Get paper that is the best size for the type of book you have chosen to make. Then neatly copy or type your story onto the paper. Use the directions for Making a Book on page 73.

6. Finally, share your finished book with the class and display it in the school library.

Editing Checklist

After writing a rough draft of your story, use this checklist (✔) to edit your work and create a better story.

_____1. What is the title of your story? Does it catch the reader's attention?

_____2. How many paragraphs does your story have? Are they indented?

_____3. The opening sentence can catch the reader's attention and encourage that person to continue reading. What is your opening sentence?

_____4. Fill in the chart below with words from your story.

NOUNS	VERBS	ADJECTIVES	ADVERBS

Did you use a variety of words?
If not, what words can you change or add to your story to give it more variety?

_____5. Well-written stories often appeal to the reader's five senses. Fill in the chart with sensory words from your story.

SMELL	HEARING	SIGHT	TASTE	TOUCH

Did you use a variety of sensory words in your story?
If not, what words can you change or add to the story to make it more interesting?

_____6. Adjectives, or descriptive words, make stories more interesting. Write down the sentence from your story that uses adjectives the most effectively.

_____7. Which sentence in your story is the most boring?

Editing Checklist *(cont.)*

Improve that sentence by elaborating or rewriting it. Now write your new and improved sentence.

_____8. What are some phrases you used to describe where your story takes place?

_____9. What are some phrases you used to describe when your story takes place?

_____10. How many times did you use the word "said"? Improve your story by using a variety of words to replace "said." Use a thesaurus for suggestions. What words did you use to replace "said"?

_____11. Look through a dictionary, thesaurus, reading textbook, or encyclopedia under a topic related to your story. See if you can find some new words that would fit into your story. List some of them below.

martin — Needs a capital letter

Dog — Needs to be lowercase letter

hungry
∧ wolf — Needs to be inserted into the word or sentence

gray gray wolf — Needs to be deleted

The gray wolf walked alone⊙ — Needs a period

wolf — Needs to be correctly spelled

_____12. Use a red pencil or pen to make the following editing marks on your rough draft.

_____13. Now neatly rewrite or type your story with all the improvements and changes you have made.

Making a Book

You can use these directions to make a book with hinged covers or a book that is like an accordion.

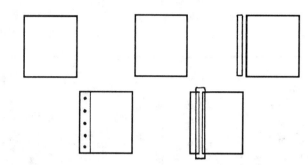

Making a Book with Hinged Covers

Materials:

> 2 pieces of posterboard or cardboard
> (cut to desired dimensions)
> clear tape
> stapler
> ½ inch (1.3 cm) wide tape

Directions:

> Step 1: Cut the cardboard or posterboard slightly larger than the story pages.
> Step 2: Cut a ½ inch strip from the left-hand side of the front cover.
> Step 3: Tape the strips together on the inside. Leave a space ⅛ inch (.32 cm) wide between the two pieces.
> Step 4: Organize your pages. Then staple the cover and the pages together.
> Step 5: Use ½ inch-wide tape to cover the front hinge, as well as the staples from the front and back.

Making an Accordion-Style Book

Materials:

> cardboard or posterboard to make a tracing pattern (cut to desired shape)
> construction paper (amount and color varies for each book)
> clear tape
> glue or stapler

Directions:

> Step 1: Pick a shape that you would like to use for your book. Draw that shape on the piece of cardboard or poster board. Then cut it out to make a tracing pattern of your shape.
> Step 2: Decide how many pages your book will need. Use the tracing pattern to cut out that number of pages from the construction paper. You can use the same color for each page, or you can use a variety of colors.
> Step 3: Lay out your pages on a table. Place your pages together as closely as possible without overlapping them.
> Step 4: Then carefully tape the pages together on the front and back.
> Step 5: Cut your writing paper to the same shape as your book, using your cardboard pattern.
> Step 6: Glue or staple your story pages to the construction paper pages. If you use glue, allow the pages to dry.
> Step 7: Fold the book like an accordion.

Be sure to include the following types of pages when you put your hinged-cover or accordion-style book together.

| front cover | title page | dedication page | story | about the author | back cover |

Research/Activity Center

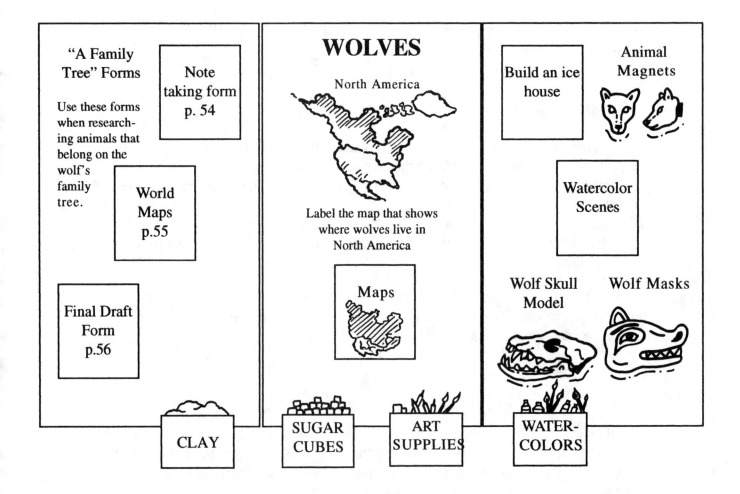

The Wolves Research/Activity Center can be set up as a bulletin board with a table in front of it or with a cardboard display on a large table. On the left side of the display, attach three large envelopes. Place the forms for "A Family Tree" (pages 53-56) in the envelopes. Display a map of North America at the top of the middle section of the display. At the bottom of this section, place an envelope with copies of the North American map that students will label (page 61). You may wish to add magazine and newspaper articles about the Arctic to this section of the display. On the right side of the displays attach copies of the directions for activities, such as "Build an Ice House" (page 16), "Wolf Masks" (page 63), "Watercolor Scenes" (page 64), "Animal Magnets" (page 65-66), and "Wolf Skull Models" (page 67). Place boxes with supplies, such as sugar cubes, general art supplies, watercolors, and clay, on the table. As students complete their wolf masks and skull models, you may wish to hang them from the ceiling above the center.

Bulletin Boards

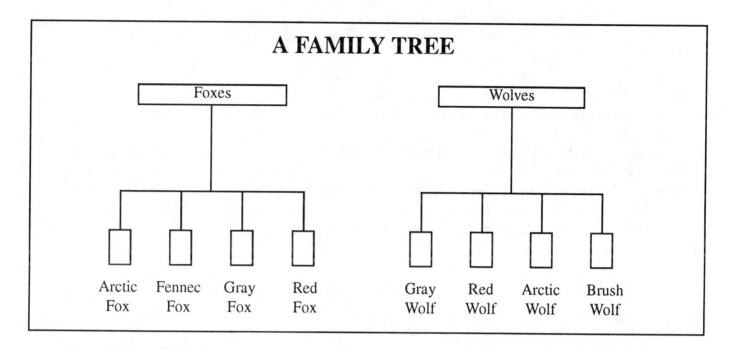

Use this bulletin board to show animals that are related to wolves. Cover the background with butcher paper or fabric. Use construction paper to create the title "A Family Tree" and the headings, such as "Foxes" and "Wolves." Have students work in cooperative learning groups to research wolves and their relatives (pages 53-56). Have students place their final drafts on the bulletin board. Use yarn or string to connect the different animals. You may wish to have students place their labeled copy of the world map under their final draft, or you can use the overhead to enlarge the map on a piece of butcher paper and have students color and label the enlarged map.

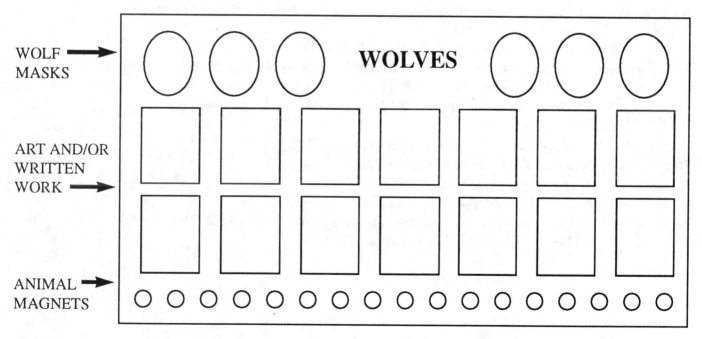

Use this bulletin board to display a variety of work, such as poetry (pages 37-39), stories (pages 40, 41, 70,) graphing activities (pages 57-58), comparisons (pages 44 and 62), and art (pages 63, 64, 65-66).

75

Bibliography

Fiction

Aiken, Joan. *The Wolves of Willoughby.* Chase, 1963.

Andrews, Jan. *Very Last First Time.* Atheneum, 1986.

Arkin, Alan. *The Learning Condition.* Harper and Row, 1976.

Calvert, Patricia. *The Hour of the Wolf.* Scribner's Books, 1983.

Gardiner, John Reynolds. *Stone Fox.* Crowell, 1980.

Houston, James. *Frozen Fire.* Atheneum, 1977.

Kjelgaard, Jim. *Big Red.* Bantam, 1945.

Mowat, Farley. *The Dog Who Wouldn't Be.* Bantam, 1957.

Mowat, Farley. *Never Cry Wolf. Bantam,* 1983.

Murphy, Jim. *The Call of the Wolves.* Scholastic, Inc., 1989.

O'Dell, Scott. *Black Star, Bright Dawn.* Houghton Mifflin, 1988.

Paulson, Gary. *Woodsong, Dogsong, and Cookcamp.* Bradbury Press, 1990.

Steiner, Barbara. *Whale Brother.* Walker and Company, 1988.

Nonfiction

Barry, Scott. *The Kingdom of the Wolves.* Putnam, 1979.

Brandenburg, Jim. *To the Top of the World: Adventures with Arctic Wolves.* Walker and Company, 1993.

Brandenburg, Jim. *White Wolf: Living with an Arctic Legend.* Northwood Press, Inc., 1988.

Cooper, Michael. *Racing Sled Dogs.* Clarion, 1988.

Field, Edward. *Eskimo Songs and Stories.* Delacorte Press, 1973.

Hansen, Rosanna. *Wolves and Coyotes.* Grosset and Dunlap, 1981.

Hinshaw, Dorothy. *Gray Wolf, Red Wolf.* Clarion, 1990.

Horowitz, Paul. *The Works of Jack London.* Avenel Books, 1980.

Hughes, Jill. *Arctic Lands.* Watts, 1987.

Johnson, Sylvia and Alice Aamodt. *Wolf Pack, Tracking Wolves in the Wild.* Lerner, 1985.

Lawrence, R.D. *Wolves.* Sierra, 1990.

Lopez, Barry Holstun. *Of Wolves and Men.* Macmillan, 1979.

Maher, Romona. *The Blind Boy and the Loon and Other Eskimo Myths.* John Day Company, 1969.

McConoughey, Jana. *The Wolves.* Macmillan, 1983.

Pelto, Pertti J. *The Snowmobile Revolution: Technology and Social Change in the Arctic.* Waveland Press, 1987.

Roever, J.M. *Endangered Animals series.* Steck-Vaughn, 1972.

Shields, Mary. *Sled Dog Trails.* Pyrola Publishing, 1984.

Thompson, Bruce. *Looking at the Wolf.* Rinehart, 1987.

Wexo, John Bonnett. *Wolves: Zoobooks 2.* Wildlife Education, Ltd., 1986.

Young, Steven B. *To the Arctic: An Introduction to the Far Northern World.* Wiley, 1989.

Yue, Charlotte and David. *The Igloo.* Houghton Mifflin, 1988.

Bibliography *(cont.)*
Video/Movies

Arctic Refuge: A Vanishing Wilderness. *60 min.* National Audubon Society, 1990.
Bering Sea: Twilight of the Alaskan Hunter. 48 min. The Cousteau Society, 1991.
Land of the Eagle. 60 min. PBS Video, 1991.
White Wolf. 60 min. National Geographic, 1989.
The Wolf: A Howling in America's National Parks. 30 min. Zion Natural History Association, 1967.
Wolves. 60 min. Vestron Video, 1989.

Teacher Resources

Adopt a Whale! For information, write to: National Wildlife Federation, Dept. 337, 1400 Sixteenth Street, N.W., Washington, DC 20036-2266.

Carolina Biological Supply Co. has endangered species board and card games. For more information, write to: Carolina Biological Supply Co., 2700 York Rd., Burlington, NC 27215.

Come with Me is a science series with educational kits and activities. One topic is Arctic Mammals of Alaska. For a catalog and more information, write to: S/S Publications Co., 3550 Durock Rd., Shingle Springs, CA 95682.

Inuit (Eskimo) alphabet posters and Inuit children posters are available free from the Department of Northern Affairs, Ottawa, Ontario, K1A OH4 Canada.

Scavengers Science Education Supply Co. has stamps, puppets, stickers, skulls, fur, and kits on Alaskan mammals. For a catalog, write to: Scavenger Science Education Supply Co.,
P.O. Box 211328, Auke Bay, AK 99821.

Wolf Song of Alaska has information about wolves. For information and a catalog, write to Wolf Song of Alaska, P.O. Box 110309, Anchorage, AK 99511-0309.

The Wolf Education and Research Center has a wolf sponsorship program. For more information write to: Wolf Education and Research Center, P.O. Box 3832, Ketchum, ID. 83340.

Computer Programs

The Balance in Nature introduces a marine environment, food chains, and survival and extinction concepts. Available from Focus Media, Inc.

Endangered Species is a four-part program involving endangered animals and decision-making skills. Available from Yaker Environmental Systems, Inc.

Voyage of the Mimi is an integrated program about whales, navigation, ecosystems, and more. Available from Holt, Rhinehart and Winston.

Answer Key

Page 11
1. Answers will vary.
2. sandpipers
   moosehide
   sealskin
   windproof
   iceberg
   fireplace
   backpack
   outdoors
   hideout
   singsong
3. Answers will vary.
4. Some possible answers include:
   pop, mom, did, gag, deed, bib, tot, pup, wow, dad, peep, Bob, noon, eve, Anna, radar, Hanna, rotor, eye, deed, sees, nun.
5. Answers will vary.

Page 13
June 21: 36 °F = 2 °C
December 21: 0 °F = -18 °C
September 21: 34 °F = -1 °C
March 21: -9 °F = -23 °C

Page 15
1. tundra
2. Eskimo
3. Inuit
4. Arctic
5. caribou
6. parka
7. lemmings
8. culture
9. cooperation
10. ajajaq

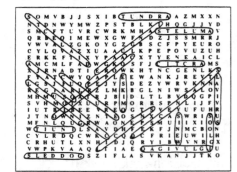

Page 24
Jack London
1. Jobs
2. San Francisco
3. Charmain
4. Klondike
5. *The Call of the Wild*
6. Orient
7. England
8. Overdose

9. Oysters
10. Thirteen

Page 25
1. A. 600 / 30 = 20 days
   B. 600 / 50 = 12 days
2. A. 14 X 40 = 560 miles
   B. 21 X 40 = 840 miles
   C. 560 / 10 = 56 miles per day
   D. 3 X 24 = 72 hours; 72 X 60 min. = 4,320 minutes
3. A. 300 X 3 ft. = 900 feet
   B. 300 X 5 sec. = 1,500 sec. 1,500 X 2 (the return trip) = 3,000 sec. or 50 min.
4. A. 50 lbs. X 20 = 1,000 lbs.
   B. 1000 lbs. / 10 = 100 sacks
   C. If that person wins: $20 X 2 = $40; If that person loses: $20.

Page 33

Crossword Puzzle

Page 36

Animal	Adaptation	Purpose of Adaptation
Lemming	-coloring	-camouflage to hide from predators
	-thick waterproof fur	-keeps warm, dry
Caribou	-short tail and ears	-conserves heat
	-wide feet	-easily runs across snow
Polar Bear	-coloring	-blends in with surroundings
	-thick, furry feet	-gives warmth, helps feet work like snowshoes
	-webbed feet	-swims easily
	-fat	-warmth, stores energy for the winter
Walrus	-thick layer of fat, or blubber	-warmth
	-tusks	-weapons, ice choppers
	-sensitive whiskers	-helps to find food in darkness
Narwhal	-oil glands in skin	-waterproof
Ptarmigan	-coloring	-camouflage
	-feathers on feet	-warmth, can shuffle through the snow
Snow Goose	-large number of feathers	-traps air for insulation
	-heavy layer of fat	-energy for migration

Page 49
1. F
2. T
3. F
4. T
5. F
6. T
7. F
8. T
9. F
10. F

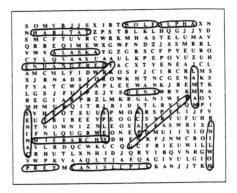

Page 50
Possible answers include:
Newborn - blind, helpless, stay in den, nurse mother's milk
11-15 days old - eyes open and are blue in color, continue to nurse mother's milk, very active in play
3-4 weeks old - emerges from den, still nurses but also eats meat brought by the pack, the pack, including the pups, leaves the area of the den to live with pack, pups learn by watching pack members
5-6 months old - loss all of it's baby teeth, hunt with the pack, weigh 45-55 lbs., has a new coat of fur
2-3 years old - fully grown, will pick a mate for life, will reproduce

Answer Key (cont.)

Pages 54

Some possible answers include:

Gray Wolf

Size: 59-80 inches long; as much as 36 inches tall; varies from 55 to 155 pounds.

Color: gray or tawny; some can be white, or black

Habitat: forests of northern North America (Alaska, Canada), and northern Asia

Food Source: deer, moose, other hoofed mammals, rabbits or rodents (if necessary), fruit and berries

Facts: Sometimes called the timber wolf; has a bad reputation in stories around the world; hunts in packs, and will track it's prey for many hours.

Red Wolf

Size: somewhat smaller than gray wolf; ranges from 55 to 80 pounds

Color: a reddish-coat with tawny muzzle and legs; can also be black

Habitat: forests of the southern United States (Louisiana, East Texas, and Arkansas)

Food Source: deer, rabbits, rodents

Facts: This wolf is on the endangered species list.

Coyote

Size 25 to 50 pounds

Color: similar to a wolf, but tawnier

Habitat: all parts of North America, from Alaska to Central America

Food Source: rabbits, rodents, and fawns (if necessary), lizards, and berries

Facts: Called the "barking dog;" famous for its evening serenade of howls; Spanish conquistadors named it from the Aztec word

"Coyotl;" Hunts in teams, instead of packs.

Jackal

Size: similar to coyotes

Color: gray, tawny, with black areas

Habitat: tropical and subtropical areas. Common jackal: southeastern Europe and Asia. Himalayan jackal: Burma and Thailand. Black-backed and Side-striped Jackals: Africa, south of the Sahara

Food Source: small mammals, vegetable matter, and carrion (dead animals)

Facts: Hunts in family groups at night; follows lions and other predators to feed on their leftovers.

Dingo

Size: similar to coyotes

Color: rusty red fur, white legs and tip of tail

Habitat: Australian bush

Food Source: kangaroos, poached mammals, rabbits, and sheep

Facts: Only wild dog that lives in Australia; Aborigines kept them as pets; The Tasmanian wolf is not a wolf but a marsupial with similar traits to the dingo.

Red Fox

Size: about 3 1/2 feet in length; 9 to 15 pounds

Color: beautiful golden-red coat, legs and tips of ears are black, tip of bushy tail is white

Habitat: forests and woods around the world

Food Source: rabbits, mice, frogs, eggs, insects, and fruit

Facts: Hunted by people in "fox hunts." Raised on farms for their coats; Can be infected with rabies.

Arctic Fox

Size: about 30 inches long; 6 to 15 pounds

Color: summer - gray, brown coats; fall - pure white to smoky blue

Habitat: tundra areas around the world

Food Source: lemmings, rodents, seabirds, eggs in the summer, scavenger in the winter

Facts: Called the white fox; Will follow polar bears in winter for seal or whale leftovers.

Fennec Fox

Size: 16 inches long, 2 to 4 pounds

Color: pale buff coat

Habitat: deserts of Northern Africa

Food Source: small rodents and insects

Facts: Has extra large ears; thought to have the most beautiful coat; the smallest of the foxes (no bigger than a rabbit)

79

Answer Key (cont.)

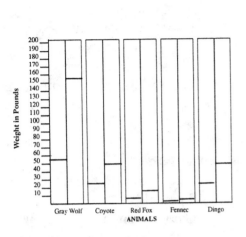

2. Answers will vary depending on graph and grid sizes.
3. Same as 2.

Use this Wolf Patern to create bulletin board and in class discussion.